ESL Composition Tales

ESL Composition Tales

Reflections on Teaching

Linda Lonon Blanton and Barbara Kroll

with
Alister Cumming
Melinda Erickson
Ann M. Johns
Ilona Leki
Joy Reid
Tony Silva

Introduction by Dana Ferris
Epilogue by Paul Kei Matsuda

Ann Arbor
THE UNIVERSITY OF MICHIGAN PRESS

Copyright © by the University of Michigan 2002
All rights reserved
Published in the United States of America by
The University of Michigan Press
Manufactured in the United States of America
⊗ Printed on acid-free paper

2005   2004   2003   2002·   4   3   2   1

A CIP catalog record for this book is available from the British Library.

Library of Congress Cataloging-in-Publication Data

Blanton, Linda Lonon, 1942–
    ESL composition tales : reflections on teaching / Linda Lonon
  Blanton and Barbara Kroll ; with Alister Cumming . . . [et al.] ;
  introduction by Dana Ferris ; epilogue by Paul Kei Matsuda.
        p.   cm.
    Includes bibliographical references and indexes.
    ISBN 0-472-08891-2 (acid-free paper)
    1. English language—Study and teaching—Foreign speakers. I.
  Kroll, Barbara.   II. Title.
  PE1128.A2   B53   2002
  428'.0071—dc21   2002006436

Preface

The various papers in Stella's desk told her that she was sixty-five. The face in the mirror . . . seemed like some disturbing distortion of her real face. . . . [M]iraculously preserved within this uncompromising prison of flesh and bone were all those other Stellas, all co-existing, all bearing witness, all available for consultation. Tell me how it was, she could say to some vanished Stella, and back would come these accounts of elsewhere and other people.—Penelope Lively, *Spiderweb*

Stella, the main character in Penelope Lively's richly textured British novel *Spiderweb,* is a newly retired social anthropologist who takes a country house and, in the process of sorting through her papers, relives her adventures, looking for her present self in the younger person she once was. Like Stella, we find ourselves gazing in the mirror and no longer seeing the youthful faces that looked back at us when we first set out on our teaching journeys. Yet beyond the outward shell remain vivid images of students we have taught, schools we have worked in, teachers we have been, co-mingling with and shaping our present teaching lives.

We find ourselves, late in our careers, looking back with wonder, curiosity, perhaps even wistfulness, reflecting on what we have learned and how we might share our cumulative learning, our insights, with others, especially younger colleagues. Reflecting on how we might bear witness. How we might make ourselves available for consultation. To past selves, we too say "tell us how it was," so we ourselves may better understand how it is. And so we tell our tales.

The genesis of this book, in itself a tale, dates to 1995, when Barbara Kroll invited several of the present contributors to join her in a reflective conversation about their lives in EFL/ESL composition teaching. They were chosen by virtue of having then 15-plus years of classroom experience and an expressed willingness to consider how (and perhaps why) their teaching methods and philosophies had changed over time.

At the 1996 TESOL conference in Chicago, Barbara served as ringmaster, opening the conversation publicly, introducing each panelist to tell a story built on the preceding one. Weaving together their stories were Ilona Leki, Joy Reid, Alister Cumming, Melinda Erickson, Ann M. Johns, and Linda Lonon Blanton. For a while after that experience, we discussed via email how to convert our separate talks into a single publishable article. None of the scenarios we came up with, however, seemed likely to preserve our individual voices and individual stories—those very aspects of our accounts that seemed the essence of what we had to say.

Publication plans went into hibernation as such things are wont to do, but we continued to discuss our stories with each other and with other colleagues whenever we met at conferences in the intervening years. Finally, Linda had the inspiration to realize that the fleshed-out versions of our stories would make for a book, and thus this collection was born. Setting out to maintain the uniqueness of each voice, we even at one point played with the metaphor of "chorale" as a frame—separate but joined in song. Although we eventually shifted to "storytelling" as a more workable metaphor, each contributor's unique style, tone, and sense of balance between personal and public will give readers, we hope, a sense of the varied lives we've led and the individuals we are. No two storytellers are alike.

To the original choir, we added Tony Silva, another long-timer in ESL/EFL composition teaching. We also decided to invite two people who represent two generations of younger (newer) scholars to complete our collection by adding book-ends to our tales: Dana Ferris to write an introduction and Paul Kei Matsuda to write an epilogue.

In recounting our stories, some of us speak primarily to

new teachers and some to more seasoned ones, but we all speak in the spirit of promoting a reflective stance. So we say, gather round, colleagues, and we shall summon vanished selves to tell you how it was, share accounts of elsewhere and other people, and remember what it once was like to teach ESL/EFL writing in the days when there were no books like this one.

Linda Lonon Blanton
Barbara Kroll

Contents

Dana Ferris, who was not even born when some of the veteran contributors to this collection began their teaching careers, is nonetheless considerably older than Paul Kei Matsuda, the other "junior" contributor, who wrote the epilogue. Starstruck while attending the 1996 TESOL colloquium, which initiated the work leading to this collection, Dana has since moved on to the more mature stage of simple respect and admiration.

Introduction

Dana Ferris
California State University, Sacramento

Beware of "complacency that puts our critical faculties to sleep."—Ilona Leki
Ask students what they want, think, and need.—Joy Reid
A "questionable practice": Error correction and identification.
—Alister Cumming
"The five-paragraph essay: Tool, or torpedo?"—Ann M. Johns
I had "a tendency to overload students."—Melinda Erickson
We need to "value qualitative research."
—Linda Lonon Blanton
"I can't believe I did that!"—Barbara Kroll

How a "New Kid on the Block" Ended Up in This Book

These wonderful "sound bites," and other provocative quotations and ideas, were swirling through my head as I left the 1996 TESOL colloquium on writing that gave rise to this collection. Like any veteran conference-goer, I have experienced papers and panels that have been good, bad, and indifferent. Over the years, I have arrived at the view that if at a professional conference I hear just one really memorable paper or colloquium panel, a presentation that stimulates or challenges my thinking or teaching, the trip is a success. I left that Chicago colloquium, orchestrated by Barbara Kroll, with a sigh of satisfaction, knowing that my modest hopes had once again been fulfilled and that the money spent, the time away (I missed my younger daughter's second birthday), and the frozen toes and fingertips (a lifelong Californian, I have limited tolerance for a Chicago winter) had been justified.

That spring semester I was teaching a graduate seminar on teaching ESL writing in the master's program in TESOL at California State University, Sacramento (CSUS). I knew my students would be eager to hear, firsthand, accounts of the veteran writing teachers and researchers whose names they had encountered in their course readings. With this in mind, I took copious notes at the colloquium, which I typed up when I got home and turned into material for my closing lecture of the course. (I also had the effrontery to throw in a few thoughts of my own.)

I called this lecture "Insights from the Leading Lights" and have since used a version of it every year. Students love it, and it always gets me an enthusiastic round of applause as I release them into the world with the final exhortation: "Go and be wonderful writing teachers." As an extrovert, of course, I thrive on this sort of affirmation, so I have been grateful to Kroll and Company ever since.

Because of my personal history with this particular panel, I was delighted when I heard about plans to turn the conference presentations into a book, and I was honored by the invitation to write the introduction to the collection. What strikes me now in reading the various contributions is the collective sense of history they convey—the history of second language teaching in general; the somewhat haphazard way in which ESL writing instruction, in particular, has evolved over the past 40 years; and especially the trends and pendulum swings that have come, gone, and come again. As Linda Lonon

Blanton and Barbara Kroll note in their preface, I am of a different generation of writing teachers from the authors whose stories appear in this volume and yet a bit further along in life and teaching than Paul Kei Matsuda, who has written the epilogue. Being in the "middle generation" of this historical progression—not among the pioneers but not among the most newly minted, either—gives me a somewhat unique vantage point. I would like to use this opportunity in the introduction to tell a bit of my own story and how the voices in this collection have influenced it and to briefly spotlight each of the various tales.

Where My Story Fits In

I entered the ESL world in 1983, at age 23, a new bride with a bachelor's degree in English (literature and creative writing) who aspired to an academic career. So I entered the brand-new master's program in TESOL at California State University, Sacramento (CSUS) (little knowing that I would, a mere seven years later, be back teaching in the same program). Even as late as the early 1980s, it was somewhat unusual to pursue TESOL training at all, and especially *before* teaching abroad, rather than afterward. I remember being quite intimidated, in my first graduate seminar, by the fact that I was almost the only student in the class with no teaching experience whatsoever. When I completed my degree in 1985, I was surprised (but pleased) to discover that teachers with degrees in TESOL were such a rare commodity that I actually had my pick of teaching jobs, despite my lack of experience. (All right, they were part-time, temporary, low-paying jobs, but still . . .)

I fell into the teaching of ESL writing as a specialty quite naturally and quite early in this process. During my first semester at CSUS, I took an internship course in which I did one-on-one tutoring in the campus writing center. Because I was in the TESOL program, the staff in the writing center was thrilled, ecstatic even, to fill my tutoring schedule with ESL students. None of the other tutors there had a clue about what to do with them. (Neither did I, actually, but at least I was learning.)

The students I worked with were mostly recent immigrants or international students from the Middle East, the Pacific Rim, and Southeast Asia. I discovered several things that semester: (1) I loved ESL students and found them fascinating; (2) I loved everything about the teaching of writing; and (3) despite my bachelor's degree with honors in English from the University of California, Davis, I knew almost nothing about writing or even about the English language. Thankfully, the professor who taught the internship course, Charles Moore (now Emeritus), was a superb teacher educator, who also had a lot of interest in and sympathy for ESL writers. I learned a lot from him about writing and about teaching.

Acting rapidly on these insights about my interests and recognizing my deficiencies, I enrolled the following semester in a class entitled "Teaching Composition in College" and another one called "Traditional Grammar and Standard Usage." In addition, I kept teaching ESL students, now in the Learning Skills Center, where I was hired as a graduate assistant (again, the only one with any TESOL training at all) to teach small-group tutorials in reading and writing. By my second year in the program, I was a teaching assistant and had my own three-unit ESL composition class to teach. By the time I completed the program, I had (for the times) an impressive record of tutoring and teaching and some very relevant and helpful coursework under my belt. The following year, I taught ESL writing courses at CSUS and at a local community college.

This resume then enabled me to qualify for a teaching assistantship at the American Language Institute (ALI) at the University of Southern California (USC), where I enrolled in

1986 to pursue a doctorate in applied linguistics (and where I was fortunate enough, like several of the other contributors to this collection, to work under the guidance of Robert Kaplan). By 1990, I was back at CSUS, teaching in the MA/TESOL program, where I am now a full professor and where I coordinate the ESL writing program for the English department. I have continued to pursue my interest in the teaching of writing through teaching ESL writing courses; regularly teaching a graduate seminar on the topic; supervising our ESL writing practicum course; conducting classroom research; and writing articles, books, and teacher-preparation materials drawn from my findings and from my own teaching experiences.

At the time I began my training and teaching career, the process approach to composition teaching had firmly taken hold in both first and second language composition circles. My graduate coursework related to writing was all heavily influenced by the then-current scholarly work of Vivian Zamel and Stephen Krashen (Krashen, 1982, 1984; Zamel, 1982, 1983, 1985). Both at CSUS and at the ALI at USC, it was a given that students should write multiple drafts of their papers, that feedback on content and form should be given at separate stages of the writing process, that grammar issues should be de-emphasized and perhaps skipped altogether, that students should collaborate in peer-feedback sessions, and that one-to-one teacher-student writing conferences were critical.

I loved teaching writing at USC. Most of the classes I was assigned were filled with fascinating international graduate students, and I enjoyed being able to just talk with them about their ideas and not worry about their language problems. After all, the most admired scholars in the field and the professors who had trained me assured me that it was not necessary *or* effective to focus on such issues. I distinctly remember marveling that I actually got paid for having such a good time.

But then the seed of doubt that this was really all there was to it was planted in me by USC professor David Eskey, in a course on teaching ESL reading and writing. Eskey's early musings on the process approach's effects on ESL writers had been captured in a brief *TESOL Quarterly* think piece, amusingly titled "Meanwhile, Back in the Real World . . ." (Eskey, 1983). In class, Eskey skillfully led us through a then-current debate among Daniel Horowitz, JoAnne Liebman-Kleine, and Liz Hamp-Lyons (Horowitz, Liebman-Kleine, & Hamp-Lyons, 1986), opening my eyes to an ESL composition world in which process really was not the only active paradigm. As I continued teaching, I became increasingly and uncomfortably aware that my students' writing problems, whether to do with form, content, or rhetoric, did not magically disappear simply because they were engaged in the writing process and given individual freedom and minimal teacher appropriation.

When I later began teaching ESL writing at CSUS, I immediately encountered the very real-world problems and challenges faced by students there. As I helplessly watched some of my own students fail the course exit exam and/or the university's writing proficiency exam (required for graduation), I began searching the literature and examining my own pedagogy for answers about how to better prepare them for the very real writing obstacles they faced. This quest was made all the more urgent by the fact that not only was I teaching my own ESL writing students but I was now training future generations of ESL writing teachers. Would I pass on and inculcate sound pedagogy and practical strategies? Or would I provide them only with vague platitudes and wishful thinking, along the lines of "Clap your hands and Tinkerbell will live again"?

As I read, thought, reflected, experimented, and researched, I became convinced of several things, but most importantly that over the history of L2 writing, every carousel horse on the "merry-go-round of approaches" (Silva, 1990, p. 18) has represented a different piece of the answer and that there is a place and context for almost every paradigm and technique.

Controlled composition? Not "real writing," of course— some would label it "writing without composing" (Grabe & Kaplan, 1996)—but potentially valuable at the beginning stages of academic writing instruction for text modeling and practice for students who are not yet fluent enough in English to produce original discourse.

Current-traditional methods? Subject to much rigidity and abuse—and subject to the worst risk, that students will be bored to death with tasks like "Write a process paragraph on how to brew a pot of coffee"—but maybe, just maybe, even a current-traditional approach carries with it some helpful tools within the notions of "thesis," "topic sentence," and "transition" that might assist emerging intermediate writers in ordering their thoughts more effectively. (Even the "five-paragraph essay"—is it a "tool or a torpedo," as Ann M. Johns asked in the colloquium? Well, it depends.) As several of the authors in this collection eloquently express, rigidity in embracing a particular paradigm and rejecting out of hand all elements of others may cause us to ignore who our students are and what they will do after we are done teaching them and to neglect good ideas that may very well be exactly what they need.

The Storytellers and Their Influence on My Own Story

The teacher-scholars whose stories and work are chronicled in this collection have been key figures in my own quest for answers over the past decade. Barbara Kroll's (1990) edited volume, *Second Language Writing,* was the textbook I adopted, along with Joy Reid's hot-off-the-press *Teaching ESL Writing* (1993), when I offered my first teacher-training course in ESL composition in the spring of 1993. (Ilona Leki's marvelous *Understanding ESL Writers,* 1992, was already in use in an internship course at CSUS, so that wasn't a possibility.) Articles and book chapters subsequently published by Johns, Kroll, Leki, Reid, and Silva have also been influential in my primary and secondary research work, my teacher-preparation courses, and my own ESL composition teaching. (I am certain that several CSUS generations of MA/TESOL students consider all five individuals as personal friends, because they have read so much of their work and heard so much about them.)

Similarly, I have become professionally acquainted over the years with Linda Lonon Blanton, Alister Cumming, and Melinda Erickson and have also found them to be wise, insightful, thoughtful, and encouraging. Every single one has been incredibly generous in their support of and interest in me as a younger, less experienced scholar in the emerging area of ESL writing. It is no wonder that I was thrilled to hear seven of them in one morning in Chicago. (The day before, I had also heard a wonderful paper by Tony Silva titled "On the Ethical Treatment of ESL Writers," later published in the *TESOL Quarterly* [Silva, 1997].)

All of the contributors to this collection (except for Paul Kei Matsuda and me, who were added as voices from "younger generations") have now taught ESL writing for 20-plus years. Here, they tell their stories in their own voices of how they came to teaching and to second language writing and of what insights they have gathered from their years of experience. The segments have in common that each is a story about more or less the same historical period. (For example, three of the authors describe using the same composition textbook in the early 1970s.) What is unique about each is the array of themes and reflections that emerge as individual narrators retrace their own footsteps.

While each story stands alone, it is also interesting to trace the connecting threads. The first three narrators, Barbara Kroll, Melinda Erickson, and Ilona Leki, detail some errors and excesses in their own careers, now seen in hindsight. Leki, Tony Silva, Joy Reid, and Ann M. Johns, though in different ways, all talk about the importance of analyzing text, context, and students themselves. In the final two tales, Alister Cumming and Linda Lonon Blanton offer critical analyses of L2 teaching and research paradigms and make recommendations and suggestions about what to avoid and how to engage in future discipline building.

An Introduction to Each ESL Composition Tale

Barbara Kroll frames her story as advice for future teachers of L2 writing. Building on her own experiences, she highlights what she specifically sees as useful: "expect the unexpected" and develop coping strategies, have confidence in the authority ascribed to you as the teacher, reflect on what you have done after the class is over, and so on. As a teacher educator, I appreciate Barbara's careful drawing out of transferable principles and strategies to help novice writing instructors learn from her experiences and even from her mistakes.

Melinda Erickson talks about "pendulum swings" that she succumbed to over time, always with the very "best of intentions." For instance, she "swung" from a tendency to overload students to a hands-off, minimalist approach. Melinda offers her experiences as "a cautionary tale" to help teachers feel better fortified to resist their own pendulum swings because of faith in their beliefs and practices. Her discussion is reminiscent of Tony Silva's (1990) description of the history of L2 writing as characterized by a "merry-go-round of approaches" that has "generated more heat than light" (18). And it reminds me of my own growing awareness that there is likely truth and value and something students need in every instructional paradigm that has ever taken root.

Next comes Ilona Leki's tale. For me, Ilona is a model of

someone who is constantly growing and discovering new things in the field; her blend of intellectual curiosity and obvious passion for discovering what is most helpful to students challenges and inspires me.

What I appreciate most about Ilona's story in this collection is the humility it embodies and calls all of us to embrace. While, like some of the other narrators, Ilona describes teaching practices that she now characterizes as excesses or mistakes, she concludes by warning us never to think that "now we know." Instead, she challenges us to constantly stay aware of research and current thinking, listen to what students tell us, listen to our own intuitions, and reflect on our teaching. Listening to her presentation in Chicago and reading her tale, I was struck by the insight that neglecting to consider any one of these three components—research, students, and our own intuitions—will put us out of balance as teachers. This is a principle I have communicated repeatedly to my own graduate students ever since.

Tony Silva was not a participant in the Chicago colloquium, but his contribution certainly belongs in this collection. His efforts, along with those of Ilona Leki, in instituting the *Journal of Second Language Writing* (*JSLW*), more than any other single achievement, established second language writing as a legitimate and important area of inquiry. Tony's own writing, dating back to the 1980s, has also been influential in advocating the uniqueness of second language writers and their ethical treatment (e.g., Silva, 1988, 1993, 1997). He also urges us to bridge the gaps between scholarship in second language writing and first language composition studies and between L2 writing and other applied linguistics subfields.

Researchers and writers in L2 composition who have benefited over the past decade from Tony's annotated bibliographies in *JSLW* (produced along with a series of graduate students, who have themselves gone on to become impressive scholars) will not be surprised to read in Tony's chapter about his devotion to spending time in the library to educate himself about L2 writing issues. The man reads everything. Also noteworthy in Tony's chapter is his extended discussion of how he has learned to always adjust his pedagogical choices to the context and needs of each new group of students, rather than relying on a textbook or assuming that we have somehow cracked the code on how to teach L2 writing and no longer have to read, reflect, or get to know our particular students.

Joy Reid's tale, which details how she has learned over her teaching career to "ask" students what they want and need, thus connects nicely with Ilona's reminder to listen to students and Tony's emphasis on adjusting our teaching strategies to each new classroom context. Though Joy is an accomplished scholar whose work has had tremendous influence on L2 writing, she is first and foremost a teacher who evidences a love for and fascination with students. She said in her 1996 conference talk that "teaching never gets boring." When you read her story, you recognize the truth of her claim. She is a teacher who is also a learner, who has deliberately put herself in the position of being instructed and informed by students. Joy's work on learning styles is another variation on the "ask" theme: Find out who the students are and how they best learn and, as a teacher, make adjustments accordingly. As a writing teacher, I am stimulated by this advice, and yet I struggle to apply it. (It is hard to let go of the notion that at least in some areas, I really do know better than my students.) Early on in my life as a parent, I read the advice to "become a student of your child." What Joy advocates in this chapter is that teachers "become students of their students."

The next narrator, Ann M. Johns, shares with Joy and Tony a passion for identifying and addressing the real-world needs of ESL writing students. I have special appreciation for Ann because, like Barbara Kroll and me, she is a faculty member in the California State University (CSU) system, a world in which teaching and administrative loads are heavy and support and rewards for research are minimal (some would say nonexistent). Despite this, she has a long and distinguished record as an incisive thinker and a superb scholar and writer. It is no exaggeration to say that when I was a new CSU professor, I literally thought: "If Ann Johns can teach in the CSU system and still be an active scholar, so can I."

In her chapter, Ann chronicles not only her evolution as a teacher but specifically why she "became an advocate for approaching writing through genre." Like all of her work, Ann's discussion of genre and ESL writing instruction is both methodically grounded in theory and scholarship *and* intensely practical in its view that writing instruction based on genre analysis is truly what is best for students facing the demands of academia and professional life.

Alister Cumming, also a pioneer in L2 writing, has made important contributions through research, mentoring of graduate students, and editorial work, especially his tenure as editor of the distinguished journal *Language Learning*. Based on the knowledge derived from scholarly endeavors and his own teaching experience, Alister identifies in his story six "principles" that he believes are valuable for the teaching of ESL writing and six "practices" that he has engaged in at various points in his career but that he now finds questionable.

To me a conference paper or a piece of writing is successful if it forces me to think critically about what is being said and if I even find myself arguing in my mind with the speaker or author. As Ilona Leki says, we are far from knowing it all about second language writing (and indeed, we probably never can or will know it all), and anything that causes us to question our own assumptions and practices has intrinsic merit. When I listened to Alister's paper in Chicago, I struggled and silently argued with several things he said. For example, I wondered why he was so negative on the issue of error correction.

In fact, Alister was editor of *Language Learning* when Truscott's (1996) controversial review essay advocating the abolishment of error correction in L2 writing classes appeared. Both Alister's conference paper and Truscott's article led to my own renewed interest in the topic and resulted in a lot of research and writing activity in that area over the subsequent years—my own and that of others (see, e.g., Ferris, 1999). As I said, provocative statements are indeed valuable if they light a fire under us and move our knowledge along.

Finally, like Alister, Linda Lonon Blanton offers suggestions for other scholars and teachers in the field of L2 writing, offered "for keeping the momentum of discipline building going." Since all of us represented in this book, along with many others, are—no question about it—engaged in the process not only of teaching ESL writing students but of building a discipline, Linda's insights offer a helpful framework for the future of L2 writing research and an appropriate conclusion to this collection.

Again, as with Alister's 1996 conference talk, I found myself arguing with Linda as she spoke, particularly on the issue of "valuing qualitative research as we have valued quantitative research." My quibble was first that I did not believe we had adequately "valued quantitative research" in L2 writing scholarship (and I would say the same for first language composition research, which can be shockingly soft as to its methodology) and that we had by no means exhausted its potential for informing us about the many questions for which we have no adequate research base. Second, I had always struggled with the tendency many scholars have to frame the distinctions between quantitative and qualitative research as a dichotomy, and a necessarily adversarial one at that (even though Linda was not framing it that way).

In my view, all research paradigms have something to offer us, and they all have significant limitations. Nonetheless,

Linda's statements forced me to clarify my own thinking about various second language–writing research paradigms—so that I could critically assess my own research designs and so that I could articulate my position in a helpful way to my graduate students, arriving at my now strongly held conclusion that the best research programs combine elements of both quantitative and qualitative research. Once again, despite my initial resistance, Linda's point of view has been formative in my own thinking, teaching, and research over the subsequent years.

Closing Thoughts

So the stories in this collection bring us "up to date" as to the history of ESL composition instruction. But this history is no dry chronology; rather, it represents the rich diversity of experiences and opinions present in our work. And within the diversity are interwoven threads as well: (1) awareness of the uniqueness of the second language writer; (2) appreciation for the insights and input of the students themselves; (3) understanding of the importance of situating L2 writing instruction within the larger social and institutional contexts in which it occurs; (4) recognition that to be the best *teachers* we can be, we must also be *thinkers and questioners;* (5) building a discipline by considering and critically analyzing the research findings not only of our contemporaries in L2 writing but of those in related fields; and (6) asking a range of questions and utilizing a range of methodologies and paradigms to investigate these questions. Finally, we must recognize that no matter which "generation" of L2 writing scholars we identify ourselves with, that generation is, as Ilona puts it, "not the end of history." And we must "guard against the complacency that puts our critical faculties to sleep" and never think "now we know it all."

References

Eskey, D. E. (1983). Meanwhile, back in the real world . . . : Accuracy and fluency in second language teaching. *TESOL Quarterly, 17,* 315–323.

Ferris, D. (1999). The case for grammar correction in L2 writing classes: A response to Truscott. *Journal of Second Language Writing, 8,* 1–11.

Grabe, W., & Kaplan, R. B. (1996). *Theory and practice of writing.* London: Longman.

Horowitz, D. M., Liebman-Kleine, J., & Hamp-Lyons, L. (1986). Two commentaries on Daniel M. Horowitz's "Process, not product: Less than meets the eye." *TESOL Quarterly, 20,* 783–798.

Krashen, S. D. (1982). *Principles and practices in second language acquisition.* Oxford: Pergamon Press.

Krashen, S. D. (1984). *Writing: Research, theory, and application.* Oxford: Pergamon Press.

Kroll, B. (Ed.) (1990). *Second language writing: Research insights for the classroom.* New York: Cambridge University Press.

Leki, I. (1992). *Understanding ESL writers.* Portsmouth, NH: Boynton/Cook Heinemann.

Reid, J. (1993). *Teaching ESL writing.* Englewood Cliffs, NJ: Regents/Prentice Hall.

Silva, T. (1988). Comments on Vivian Zamel's "Recent research on writing pedagogy." *TESOL Quarterly, 22,* 517–519.

Silva, T. (1990). Second language composition instruction: Developments, issues, and directions in ESL. In B. Kroll (Ed.), *Second language writing: Research insights for the classroom* (pp. 11–23). Cambridge: Cambridge University Press.

Silva, T. (1993). Toward an understanding of the distinct nature of L2 writing: The ESL research and its implications. *TESOL Quarterly, 27,* 657–677.

Silva, T. (1997). On the ethical treatment of ESL writers. *TESOL Quarterly, 31,* 359–363.

Truscott, J. (1996). The case against grammar correction in L2 writing classes. *Language Learning, 46,* 327–369.

Zamel, V. (1982). Writing: The process of discovering meaning. *TESOL Quarterly, 16,* 195–209.

Zamel, V. (1983). The composing processes of advanced ESL students: Six case studies. *TESOL Quarterly, 17,* 165–187.

Zamel, V. (1985). Responding to student writing. *TESOL Quarterly, 19,* 79–102.

Barbara Kroll was too young to drive when she rode a bicycle to her first teaching assignments as a French tutor to fellow high-school students in Brooklyn. Following a brief foray into journalism and public relations, she became an EFL teacher in Israel in the early 1970s, immediately recognizing that teachers could benefit from training. In fall 2001, she taught freshman composition to ESL students for the first time in 10 years, immediately recognizing that teachers are always in training.

What I Certainly Didn't Know When I Started

Barbara Kroll
California State University, Northridge

> *You can't know what you haven't had time to learn yet. You can't know what you haven't taken the time to learn yet. But you can know that there are things to learn.*—Kroll's Axiom (1989)

It is, of course, axiomatic that teachers just starting out simply cannot have had the time to complete their learning, impatient as they may be to know everything in advance of their first teaching assignment. Perhaps the most appropriate metaphor for the process of gaining the knowledge necessary for successful teaching is, in fact, that of a lifelong journey in which the final destination can *never* be reached. But I would like to think that, had there been books such as this one in the beginning of my now-long teaching career, there are things I might have learned earlier on or at least been able to think through with greater clarity. I recognize that many novice teachers experience their early teaching encounters with a great deal of angst, as did I. And I can only hope that the tales in this collection might serve to validate the reality of their experiences and sharpen their insight on how to work toward mastery of their craft.

I guess what I certainly didn't know when I started was that the most valuable tool in my personal evolution from novice to veteran teacher would not prove to be a miracle textbook or a singularly obvious pedagogy or a theory to conveniently explain all of the variables I had to deal with. (Of course, these three were the Holy Grail that I spent my energies alternately searching and praying for.) No, the most valuable tool would be the sharing of experience and insight to help guide me on my teaching journey, the treasures of accumulated wisdom sometimes referred to as "lore" (to say nothing of what has now become an ever-expanding body of published research).

As this sharing of information came to me gradually in informal and formal meetings with colleagues, I came to recognize that I belonged to a community of like-minded teachers who were working in some grand collective way (though often from very different perspectives) to find the best ways to reach students. The voices of a number of such teachers are heard in this volume, each providing a tale in his or her way that demonstrates a commitment to the continuing ability to grow.

Expecting the Unexpected

After many years as an instructor of ESL/EFL in general and ESL composition in particular, I became a teacher trainer, also now many years ago. Since then, on my campus, I have had the opportunity to offer graduate seminars for the master's degree students in English selected to teach freshman composition. And, as part of our graduate program in linguistics with a TESL/TEFL emphasis, I also teach courses in issues related to the teaching of reading and writing to L2 students.

As Penny Ur, teacher trainer extraordinaire, rather diplomatically pointed out at the 1998 TESOL conference in Seattle, teacher trainers often have no training to *be* trainers but rather may be "elevated" to their positions simply as a result of having garnered a certain amount of teaching experience (Ur, 1998). Exactly my case. Since I had no direct training to be a composition or an ESL/EFL instructor when I first began teaching those subjects either, being cast in the role of teacher trainer with no particular training to undertake that kind of teaching didn't feel all that unusual to me at the time.

I have, however, long since become a great believer in the value and power of training. It now seems to me not only foolhardy but inexcusably irresponsible for new teachers to begin their teaching journeys, as did I, with no understanding of what to expect or how to prepare themselves. As for me, what *was* I thinking? What were those who hired me thinking? Surely dealing with the complex and interacting dynamics of subject-matter material, students, classroom situations, and institutional demands requires far more than youthful enthusiasm and good will, or zeal and "the best of intentions," as Melinda Erickson so aptly puts it in her tale.

Still, as a composition teacher trainer, I sometimes feel embarrassed when novice teachers under my supervision seem to assume that (*a*) I never made the classroom gaffes I witness them commit on the very day I observe their classes; or (*b*) I have just the right technique to get sullen Natasha interested, withdrawn Hiroshi to participate, and confrontational Reza to stop acting out; or (*c*) I could easily generate an ironclad, foolproof, guaranteed-to-succeed syllabus that would put theirs to shame; or (*d*) all of the above.

Nothing could be further from the truth. I could regale my teachers in training with anecdotes about classroom gaffes, unresponsive students, and ill-conceived syllabus choices. I too have put my students into groups, set them to doing a task, and then discovered after 10 minutes that it was far too difficult and/or the directions were much too opaque to follow. I too have observed students without book or notebook, scrunched down in their seats, who indirectly challenge me to bring them into the moment. I too have had to distribute a revised syllabus halfway through the term, dropping some of the readings and adding more explanatory material about how to fulfill tasks and requirements needed to complete the course successfully. And these examples could just as easily have come from last term as from my early days of teaching. Alas.

In fact, to reduce my 34 years in the classroom to a single lesson, I'd have to paraphrase the title of a Donald Murray (1989) book and say that the lesson is to expect the unexpected. What many years of teaching have taught me is that when things go awry—when the unexpected does occur—with a lesson, a student, an assignment, a plan of study, I will find a way to regroup, reorganize, and restore my students and the course to operating on an even keel with little or no loss to my credibility as instructor. I will not feel what I used to feel as a novice teacher—that the situation is beyond repair or it is the students' faults or the book's fault, and there is nothing I can do about it. I will not feel destroyed, defeated, deflated—in short, a complete failure (or, at least, not for very long).

But, to be honest, the ability to believe that something going wrong was neither the end of the world nor proof positive that I could not teach did not come quickly or easily. One key goal for me now in training new teachers is to find ways to shorten the time they will need to teach before they begin to feel confident of their own coping strategies. Knowing what to expect, how to plan for a course, and how to interact with students certainly contributes to building this confidence.

Understanding Teaching

One of the first things candidates for the TA training program on my campus want to know is what textbook they will be using with which to "deliver" the freshman composition course. I empathize with their belief that the materials for this course—in fact, its very definition—will be encased in a book, which, if studied zealously and "learned," will prepare them for their first term of teaching.

I once held fast to this very notion about textbooks myself. To use Tony Silva's phrase (as amplified in his tale), I was "textbook bound." When I taught my first college class, I had a bachelor's and a master's degree in hand, but I had zero coursework related to pedagogy or practice. Nor did I pass through any kind of assistantship or supervised teaching experience as so many graduate students do today. In retrospect, though, I do not think the underlying message in that model was that "anyone can teach," an interpretation some might be tempted to make in an analysis of the times. Rather, the message was, I think, that teaching was *not* about what took place between student and teacher—the classroom dynamic, as it were—but about the *content* in the teacher's head.

You see, we subscribed then to the "banking model" of education (Freire, 1970), in which an advanced degree attested to vast quantities of "deposits" that had been made and teaching simply required "withdrawals" of various bits and pieces to deposit into someone else's head. Given such a model, textbooks could be seen as the central depository—that is, a distillation of the most necessary content. Thus, it is not surprising that what I wanted to do as a new teacher was to look for materials *outside* the classroom to package as lessons (i.e., materials found in books). It took many years before I came to appreciate the ample material *inside* the classroom—namely the students.

And there is so much to be learned from our very own students. This is a theme running through nearly all of the stories in this book, and especially in the tale told by Joy Reid. The longer one teaches, the more it becomes obvious that students are a much better resource than textbooks. For me, a turning point came after several years of teaching, when I was required to conduct individual conferences with ESL students in my freshman composition classes during the first year of my doctoral studies. While I have always been the sort of teacher to engage in conversation with my students and even to socialize with groups of them on occasion, it simply had never occurred to me to consult them about their experiences *as* students, as learners in *my* classes.

In my first round of face-to-face conferences, it was astonishing for me to hear students' interpretations of my assignments, hear their rationales for choices they made in their writing (often resulting in unintended poor writing), and then hear suggestions—made perhaps timidly—that we change some classroom procedure. It didn't take me long to realize that students had far more to teach me about how to help them than any textbook possibly could. When you are new to teaching, failure to consider your students as a resource results from lack of awareness (or lack of training). When you are an experienced teacher, such a failure, I believe, amounts to arrogance.

I do not mean to imply that all (let alone some) students in all (let alone one) context(s) will necessarily be able to articulate what it is they need to learn, nor will they necessarily be able to make concrete and valid suggestions on how best to structure a course to help them grow as writers. But students are the real stakeholders in our teaching lives, and it is important for teachers to find ways to "hear" even silent students.[1] We teachers spend a lot of our professional lives talking *about* students, mostly to other teachers (see, e.g., Helmers, 1994), and of course, talking *to* them, but we need to spend more time talking *with* them.

Changing Notions of Authority

My very first college job, in 1967, was teaching a night section of freshman composition at my alma mater, Brooklyn College. (This was a moonlighting position, as I had a full-time day job in public relations—the area related to my master's degree in mass communications.) I was desperate to hide from students the fact that I had no training to teach (see Kroll, 2001), since, in my mind, that meant I had absolutely no authority to be in the classroom.

Authority had a very narrow range of meaning for me at the time, and it came from a definitive knowledge about what to do in the classroom, or so I believed, and not from the simple but incontrovertible fact that I was listed on the roster as the instructor of record.[2] Nowadays, I tell my first-time teachers that a certain mantle of authority is most assuredly confirmed by the act of being named "teacher" and that they *will* grow into a deeper sense of authority. But I suspect they don't exactly believe me.

In this first teaching position, I used the very reader that my own much-beloved freshman composition instructor had used, and my general game plan was to re-create lessons that were as close as possible to what I remembered my secret mentor having done. We worked our way through the semester by reading "great essays" of the Western world, discussing them to demonstrate the ability to engage in esoteric and weighty discussions, and writing about them from a distanced and philosophical perspective. (In short, B-O-R-I-N-G.) To this textbook of essays was added a required rhetoric textbook whose lessons emphasized that student writers should aim for essays that had "unity," "coherence," and "emphasis," a trio whose meanings I struggled to understand myself, though I repeatedly tossed these words out to students as if their properties were self-evident (an experience not unlike Ilona Leki's struggle with "thesis statement," as recounted in her tale).

I felt triumphant once I'd memorized the terms so I could appear as the authority who knew what good writing was: writing that had U, C, E (*U*ncle *C*harles's *E*ducation being my mnemonic). Advice from hindsight: Don't throw terms at your students that you don't understand and/or that don't make sense to you. Don't be afraid to share your own doubts about the usefulness of claims made by books you didn't write.

Though I greatly admired and respected my own freshman composition teacher, I could no more have brought myself to consult her then about my teaching than I could imagine going to the Pope if I happened to be Catholic and were worried about my religious practice. I considered her as infallible an authority on teaching as I presume the Pope to be in his realm: not just anyone can approach them. At the time, I imagined that going to her would be revealing myself as the fraud I knew I was, and the greatest fear I had was not of failure but of being outed as a fraud. From my veteran-teacher perspective today, I can say that I hope novice instructors will have the foresight to realize that they should not confuse inexperience with fraudulence. They should never be afraid to consult with more experienced teachers when there is reason to value their input. (And see again Kroll's Axiom, at the beginning of this chapter, from Kroll, 1989.)

For the entire 15-week term of that first semester of teaching (and even for the next term as well), I entered each class in a high state of anxiety, certain that that evening would finally be the one in which the charade would be over. Like the ending of the *Wizard of Oz,* the curtain would be pulled back and there would be no wizard: the person known as "teacher" would be revealed as having no game plan, no awareness of what "philosophy of teaching" possibly meant, nor any notion of how to assess student progress, even assuming that this person recognized that a key goal in composition instruction was precisely for students' writing to progress.

Prior to each class, I jotted down notes about the sequence of what I planned to do, for without the notes to remind me of my plans, I was not sure how I would survive, given my extreme state of nervousness. Furthermore, after each class, I took the time to mark down on these notes what I had worn to class. I was certain that if I varied my wardrobe for my twice-a-week class, students would somehow recognize that I was a person of authority. As if they noticed. As if they would remember. I equated my authority with students' respect for me as a person who knew exactly what she was doing—a troubling proposition given that they were almost all older than I (read: they had more life experience) and that I was an extremely young-looking 22-year-old, still living with my parents (subtext: I was just a kid).

It didn't occur to me that writing down what happens after a class is over and reflecting on what might have been done differently or even what worked especially well is one of the most important training tools new teachers can develop on their own. More than wardrobe notes, brief notes about what went on in class would have gone a long way to making my next few terms of teaching more fruitful. Somehow I imagine that my own freshman composition teacher, who had us keeping introspective journals back in 1962, would have counseled me to write those after-class observations had I gotten up my nerve to go and speak to her at the time.

Today I work with novice teachers, not only coaching them to keep reflective, post-teaching logs but also helping them to see how each choice made in the classroom speaks to a particular philosophy of teaching and works to shape the course as a whole. Each choice should be carefully thought through both before and *after* class.

Stumbling into EFL

My formative experiences in teaching composition to non-native speakers of English took place in Beersheba, Israel, in the early 1970s, at a then brand-new university, later to be named Ben-Gurion University of the Negev (BGU), in the heart of the desert.[3] Following the British model, students at

BGU majored in a single subject area, and my affiliation was to an English department, where most of the students enrolled were planning to become English teachers in the Israeli school system. Coursework for these students consisted of separate classes in literature, linguistics, and language. The language teachers' job was to provide a six-hour-a-week course in grammar, reading, and composition to students in their first, second, and third (final) years of study, somewhat as a "service" component to the "real" courses in literature and linguistics. (Do things ever change when it comes to the politics of composition?)

Several native speakers of English from a variety of English-speaking countries and backgrounds were assembled as the service faculty, the minimum requirement being that we hold a master's degree. Few of us had much in the way of real qualifications, apart from our fierce devotion to Israel at the time. The fact that my master's degree was in mass communications and not in English or linguistics was deemed less significant than the fact that I was a native speaker of English. In fact, I did not even know what linguistics was. Further, having had the experience of teaching five composition courses on American soil put me in the position of being assigned as the "expert" to teach composition to the few native speakers of English who enrolled in the new English degree program. Mostly, however, I was hired to teach English to non-native speakers of English, an area in which I had no experience (or training).

Washed up among us was a British man who had taught English in Africa and Asia for many years. I say "washed up" purposefully, for Laurence Levine (a pseudonym) was as separate from the rest of us as would be an alien species of fish that had washed up on a distant beach, with its lifeblood ebbing away, deprived of its familiar elements and surrounded by local sea life that was strangely capable of being fully at home on the sand as well. Laurence was closer to the end of his career than to the beginning, his interest in Israel appeared to be nonexistent, and his apartment was as close to the style of a Japanese flat as he was able to create in Beer-sheba, down to the silk kimonos he donned for faculty meetings. And we met often at Laurence's place, since his extensive teaching experience gave him not only seniority but also the credibility that the rest of us lacked. He was placed in charge of creating the bulk of the materials we used in class, materials filled with references to obscure and often unpronounceable geographical locations in unknown and distant lands to which Laurence retained enormous allegiance. (And how he loved to taunt the American secretary for her misspellings of these unknown places as she typed up the materials for mimeograph duplication.)

Not surprisingly, given the times (the early 1970s), Laurence believed that grammar was the key to language learning. In fact, Linda Lonon Blanton's chapter reviews the circumstances that led to an obsession with grammar and serves to place Laurence squarely at the center of his historical context. Still, the result was that I found myself teaching grammar from Laurence's homegrown materials, using a drill-based approach that I found dreadfully tedious.

In truth, my distaste for these materials was based not only on their discrete-point approach but on the fact that the "content," or subject matter, of individual sentences was filled with references to Laurence's own personal experiences and life history, which were as far removed from our students' lives as they were from my own. I thought it terribly distasteful to thrust one's egomania so strongly in the face of students. But since our students took a common final that included a grammar test devised by Laurence, we needed to teach them to write error-free sentences and detect and analyze grammar errors in ways that Laurence had decreed. As educators elsewhere today no doubt still debate the merits of "teaching to the test," my colleagues and I certainly argued about such an approach in numerous heated faculty meetings, accompanied by pots of Japanese green tea served by Laurence to assuage our tempers. It should not be surprising that the "pot of tea" I serve my future teachers today is a thorough discussion of assessment issues and how they interact with and even shape curriculum choices, not always in positive ways.

Nevertheless, at that time and for whatever reasons, I really bought into the idea that error was bad. Any error was bad, all errors were equally bad, and every error must be eradicated if students were to be taken seriously as speakers/users of English. While I had no idea of the rationale behind this—never having heard of the behaviorist approach, which purported to explain why practice was so important— I probably thought that errors were definitive proof of poor learning.[4]

Thankfully, second language acquisition theory (SLA) has since moved front and center into language-teacher training, and few newly minted ESL/EFL teachers today are as naive about the nature of learning as was I. That errors are developmentally inevitable is a primary lesson that research on learning now offers teachers in training, and this insight leads to a far different response to deviations from standard English. Like so many components of the teaching equation that once seemed straightforward, issues related to error correction are far from simple, as Alister Cumming so clearly points out in this collection and as Dana Ferris has written about so compellingly elsewhere (Ferris, 1999).

Our desert faculty discouraged extensive writing, for the longer students' essays were, the more errors they were likely to make—proof positive they had not mastered English. Writing was seen as grammar in practice, and without the ability to "do" grammar, students had no reason to write full-length papers. The remedy for their problems wasn't to have them rewrite their papers, let alone correct individual sentences (methods that later came to be popular), but to ply them with more grammar.

The backbone of grammar instruction was sentence drills—isolated, decontextualized sentences demonstrating the right way to use the past tense, the right way to structure subordinate clauses, and so on, followed by sentences to practice on. This was the heart of Laurence's materials, and his idea of lessening the tedium was to pack sentences with what he perceived to be interesting tidbits of information, along with "in" jokes (that left virtually all of us out).

But without context, I later realized, it simply was unlikely that students would hook into the underlying linguistic principles at work, internalize them, and apply them to their own use of the language. We believed that the goal of grammar instruction was to provide knowledge that would create improved grammar "performance," but we truly didn't understand that we were providing knowledge *about* grammar and not a path toward improved *skill in* grammar.

As for writing, Laurence insisted that first-year students be limited to writing one-paragraph essays, since that gave them more than ample room to demonstrate their grammatical competence, or more likely, the lack thereof. Nothing could be gained, he reasoned, by asking them to write anything longer than that, since they would simply make more mistakes. Limiting writing to a single paragraph meant severely limiting the range of topics that could be developed in just a few sentences. We mostly worked toward five-sentence paragraphs: an opening "thesis" statement, followed by three sentences to develop the thesis, and ending with a single-sentence summary or conclusion. If this sounds remarkably like the five-paragraph essay, shrink-wrapped to fit a single paragraph, then by Jove, you've got it!

Having jumped aboard this "accuracy is all" bandwagon, I devoted my energies to dreaming up topics that would interest students, often presenting them with the opening sentence myself, written so they could easily generate the rest of the paragraph, or so I thought. These scaffolds would allow them to concentrate on the important stuff—getting their sentence-level grammar right. Those who turned in paragraphs that most closely matched the expectations I had in mind when I created the frame for the topic got the highest marks and the strongest praise. It did not occur to me that I was actually *preventing* students from progressing in their writing by so rigidly controlling their output.

I recognize a similar impulse in the novice teachers I supervise when they devise activities that march their students through some narrow lockstep procedure that yields exactly what they are looking for. They feel deflated when I tell them that their "fantastic" lesson plan might not, when all is said and done, be worth recycling in later semesters. Teaching, I tell them, is not about feeding a teacher's sense of accomplishment but about giving students tools or a sense of mastery to engage in tasks *they* want to undertake.

Enter Rhetoric

Within the first year of teaching in Israel, it became clear to me—and to most of my fellow language teachers—that students even in the same year of study exhibited varying skill levels and that one size, at best, only fit some. My work with the native English speakers also put me in a position of wanting to work with the most advanced L2 students, and addressing their writing needs meant requiring them to write full-length essays. And, given my attitude toward textbooks and my experience teaching composition in the U.S., I yearned for a book that would guide me in teaching these more advanced students to write. In fact, I was a slavish devotee of textbooks, and no textbook was more lovingly clutched in my hands than Bander's *American English Rhetoric* (1971), discussed in some detail in Ann M. Johns's tale in this collection as well.

Bander's textbook was specifically designed to teach composition to non-native speakers of English, with a focus on full-length essays, and its underlying premise was that student writers needed to practice and learn *patterns* of exposition. (Pattern-practice-for-sentences being replicated as pattern-practice-for-essays was completely lost on me at the time.) This was familiar stuff, for Bander presented patterns not unlike those that were then commonly found in writing textbooks for American college students, an early example of how L2 composition pedagogy was firmly rooted in L1 composition pedagogy.

Even though Uncle Charles's Education (you remember: *unity, coherence,* and *emphasis*) did not appear in Bander, other terms I'd embraced back in the States *were* there for me to recycle: *classification, comparison and contrast, cause and effect,* and so on. But unlike in the American textbooks, where essays illustrating rhetorical principles were written at several levels of stylistic sophistication above the competence of even stellar students, the essays in Bander were simplified, probably designed to represent a kind of writing the author thought EFL students were capable of producing if they adhered to the fairly rigid formulae he (and I, as his willing disciple) promoted.

While I can't be sure it was in Bander, I do remember reading a fascinating essay about a novel written in the very early twentieth century about an unsinkable ship that hit an iceberg and sank on its maiden voyage. The essay went on to draw comparisons to the historical events surrounding the building and sailing of the *Titanic* some years later and to show how the novelist had written a book that foreshadowed the whole disaster. That this factoid embedded itself in my long-term memory demonstrates how intensely I must have encouraged my students to engage with those textbook essays. In fact, my enthusiasm for such "sample" essays hooked me on Bander's textbook.

I was so taken by how much more interesting it was for students to read texts like this than Laurence's decontextualized sentences that I failed to notice how formulaic they were as models, how stultifyingly similar the students' own essays were in response, and how devoid of voice was the writing these fake essays generated. In fact, I failed to notice this for quite some time. A decade later, as an instructor then in an intensive English language institute in California, I was still happily using form-based approaches to teach writing to students at lower proficiency levels than Bander's audience (see Arnaudet & Barrett, 1981; Oshima & Hogue, 1983), still believing that form should be the main concern of novice and L2 writers.[5]

Thoroughly believing in the supremacy of rhetorical modes might now seem an embarrassment, given my own and our profession's rejection of formulaic and rigid form-driven approaches to writing, but it did indirectly lead me to a life-changing experience. In the introduction to Bander, I had found a distilled version of Kaplan's (1966) introduction to contrastive rhetoric, complete with the original doodle drawings—Kaplan's work apparently having had a great impact on Bander. After a few years of teaching in Israel, and growing in the recognition that I wanted to pursue doctoral studies in teaching second language writers, I discovered that Kaplan—whom I'd met through Bander, so to speak—was based at the University of Southern California (USC).

USC had just started a new interdisciplinary doctoral program in rhetoric, linguistics, and literature, which I was thrilled to be accepted into. Anticipating that I would return to Israel as a fully trained (and thus "real") teacher, I left in 1974 to pursue my doctorate full-time, an experience that didn't play itself out quite as anticipated (see Kroll, 2001). I did, however, go on to earn a Ph.D. in applied linguistics at USC, undertaking studies both in second language acquisition and rhetoric.

It was, however, the work of an L1 composition scholar, and not my early studies in SLA, that led me to recast my attitude toward error. I can almost recall the sweaty palms, the racing heartbeat, and flushed feeling of near nausea that came over me just a few years into my studies when I read Shaughnessy's *Errors and Expectations* (1977). Recognizing that my belief system was being shattered, I went into a physical panic as I began to fathom how little I really understood about the native-Hebrew-speaking students I had spent four years teaching. In explaining *why* basic writers write the way they do, Shaughnessy says:

> . . . a closer look will reveal very little that is random or "illogical" in what they have written. And the keys to their development as writers often lie hidden in the very features of their writing that English teachers have been trained to brush aside with a marginal code letter or a scribbled injunction to "Proofread!" (p. 5)

From reading Shaughnessy, I realized the obvious: that students were complex sentient beings who often had very well-thought-out reasons they could readily articulate for making the very linguistic choices that led them to error's doorstep. I found that studying rhetoric in conjunction with linguistics at that particular time provided me an optimum opportunity to consider the many ways in which the teaching of writing to second language writers draws from both areas, an opportunity few of my cohorts had. As linguistics students, we learned about the systematicity of language, and in our applied strand, we focused on how to transmit knowledge about the systems of English to an audience of English language learners. But this told us little about writing beyond the sentence level. Only from my studies in rhetoric was I able to learn how to identify textual properties that contribute to proficiency in writing and to learn about such key constructs as audience and purpose in writing.

While a TA in graduate school, I taught freshman composition sections designated for international students and then moved on to a series of mostly temporary teaching appointments until I secured a tenure-track appointment. I continued to work with ESL writers in a variety of settings and, as in the stories my colleagues tell in this collection, moved through a series of methodologies that seemed to ripple through the field—some adapted from L1 practices (e.g., a focus on personal expression) and some more suited to L2 students (e.g., content-based instruction). I realized that my classes were beginning to have no resemblance to the classes I had taught 10 years earlier and, soon enough, 20 years earlier.

By the early 1990s, the ongoing change for me was the growing realization—one I had been slow to come to—that the overwhelming majority of ESL students at my now-permanent home institution were not at all like the ESL students I had perhaps finally learned to teach. For I had cut my teaching teeth on "foreign" ESL students, those who had done a majority of schooling in their home countries and who were in the U.S. as foreign visa students with the intention of returning home. The fact is that the ESL students I now deal with are primarily immigrants, students who have completed a majority of their education in the United States, the group now labeled "Generation 1.5" (see Harklau, Losey, & Siegal, 1999). So, even though I might have thought I had gotten my belief system in order and assembled a repertoire of workable practices, this is a whole different population that I must now learn to work with in ways I have not yet mastered (see again Kroll's Axiom). This time, however, I know, at the very least, that it is not a textbook that will help me find ways to help my students. Rather, it is the students themselves who will help me, along with colleagues who continue to share their own accumulated wisdom.

A Role for Training

While all of us inevitably are inexperienced when we first start teaching, it is not the case that we know nothing about teaching, any more than a first-time parent knows nothing about raising children. Our lives as students serve as an indirect apprenticeship, since we have spent thousands of hours in the presence of teachers and teaching, hours that shape our perceptions of how we conduct ourselves in the classroom and that add up to a kind of training.[6]

Many college teachers have a history that parallels mine. My first teaching appointment started without my having taken a single course in pedagogy or having had a single hour of coaching or instruction for my new duties. Still, I had been a student for 17 years and was not without some understanding of the craft of teaching. Understandably, I tried to re-create the classrooms of the teachers I most admired. But this is not an optimum path, and I do not recommend it to others.

There is no longer any excuse to accumulate a storehouse of memories that will simply serve to show, as their careers reach their middle years, what teachers didn't know when they started. I strongly recommend that all new teachers engage in a period of formal training. It is not a substitute for teaching experience but a way to make early experiences more meaningful. Formal training would have shortened the time it took me to come to learn what experience eventually was able to teach me. This is not to say that my training is over just because I can point to my experience(s) as a teacher. Training is not something that ends when one finishes a particular course of study or a period of apprenticeship under the supervision of an experienced mentor. Every class I teach and every student I interact with creates an additional opportunity for training, learning, and growing.

It is my hope that this tale and the tales of my veteran colleagues will help all teachers—those starting their careers and those further along the way—to go (back) to their class-rooms more inquisitive about the choices they make and with a renewed enthusiasm for learning.

Notes

1. Wendy Bishop points out that L1 writing researchers also have been known to overlook the importance of consulting with the very students they study and write about. She finds these "student-vacant" reports (Bishop, 1993, p. 197) sometimes draw erroneous conclusions about such things as students' emotions and their relationship to their writing tasks.

2. For a brief discussion of multiple meanings of *authority,* see the entry in Heilker and Vandenberg (1996). For multiple views on the term as seen through the perspective of today's graduate students, see the four papers that constitute chapter 4 ("What about Authority?") in Good & War-shauer (2000).

3. My move to Israel was undertaken for a host of personal reasons, and my intended goal was to continue my career in public relations. My decision to secure a full-time teaching appointment occurred rather reluc-tantly, after I had tried in vain for nearly a year in Israel to secure a job in what I saw as my real field, namely communications. For more on this part of my story, including a discussion of how and why I switched careers as a result of moving to Israel, see Kroll (2001).

4. For a solid discussion of behaviorism and its connection to lan-guage-teaching philosophies, see Linda Lonon Blanton's chapter in this vol-ume.

5. In using the Internet to track down the publishing information for Bander's (1971) text, I discovered that as recently as fall 1998, a professor of English in Korea was still using the 1978 edition of Bander's book as a course text. Form-focused writing instruction may well have a place for cer-tain writers in certain circumstances.

6. I owe this insight to Donald Freeman of the School for International Training in Vermont, who spoke about it many years ago at a national TESOL convention.

References

Arnaudet, M. L., & Barrett, M. E. (1981). *Paragraph development: A guide for students of English as a second language.* Englewood Cliffs, NJ: Prentice Hall.

Bander, R. G. (1971). *American English rhetoric.* New York: Holt, Rinehart, Winston.

Bishop, W. (1993). Students' stories and the variable gaze of composition research. In S. I. Fontaine & S. Hunter (Eds.), *Writing ourselves into the story: Unheard voices from composition studies* (pp. 197–214). Carbondale: Southern Illinois University Press.

Ferris, D. (1999). The case for grammar correction in L2 writing classes: A response to Truscott. *Journal of Second Language Writing, 8,* 1–11.

Freire, P. (1970). *Pedagogy of the oppressed.* New York: Continuum.

Good, T. L., & Warshauer, L. B. (Eds.). (2000). *In our own voice: Graduate students teach writing.* Needham Heights, MA: Allyn & Bacon.

Harklau, L., Losey, K. M., & Siegal, M. (Eds.). (1999). *Generation 1.5 meets college composition: Issues in the teaching of writing to U.S.-educated learners of ESL.* Mahwah, NJ: Lawrence Erlbaum Associates.

Heilker, P., & Vandenberg, P. (Eds.). (1996). *Keywords in composition studies.* Portsmouth, NH: Boynton/Cook Heinemann.

Helmers, M. H. (1994). *Writing students: Composition testimonials and representations of students.* Albany: SUNY Press.

Kaplan, R. B. 1966. Cultural thought patterns in intercultural education. *Language Learning, 16,* 1–20.

Kroll, B. (1989, December). On becoming an ESL writing teacher, Plenary Talk, Symposium on Culture, Writing, and Related Issues in Language Teaching, Georgia State University, Atlanta.

Kroll, B. 2001. The composition of a life in composition. In T. Silva & P. Matsuda (Eds.), *On second language writing* (pp. 1–16). Mahwah, NJ: Lawrence Erlbaum Associates.

Murray, D. M. (1989). *Expecting the unexpected. Teaching myself—and others—to read and write.* Portsmouth, NH: Boynton/Cook Heinemann.

Oshima, A., & Hogue, A. (1983). *Writing academic English.* Reading, MA: Addison-Wesley.

Shaughnessy, M. P. (1977). *Errors and expectations. A guide for the teacher of basic writing.* New York: Oxford University Press.

Ur, P. (1998, March). Functions of the EFL teacher trainer. Paper presented at the 32nd Annual TESOL Convention, Seattle, WA.

Melinda Erickson has been a teacher most of her life—giving piano lessons to neighborhood children, tutoring English to students in France, teaching ESL to university students in California, conducting teacher-training courses in Beijing, or teaching composition to multilingual undergraduates in Berkeley. Throughout her career she has tried to improve as a teacher, most recently by trying to resist internal pendulum swings.

The Best of Intentions

Melinda Erickson
University of California, Berkeley

I began teaching second language composition to ESL students in 1979 as a teaching assistant at the University of California at Los Angeles (UCLA). What were my qualifications? I had earned a TESL Certificate from UCLA the previous year. But even though the program did offer composition pedagogy as an elective, it was not a course I had chosen. Ironically, I assumed that teaching writing must be fairly straightforward, the same way many people think that teaching their native language should be easy. I also assumed that this important work would be simple, as long as I planned well, loaded my students with information in class and in individual conferences, and responded to their essays by commenting on everything I noticed. Since my TESL Certificate program certainly did not teach me that, I can only attribute these assumptions to my initial zeal. I lacked experience, but I definitely looked forward to my first class with the best of intentions.

In 1996, when Barbara Kroll invited me to join the TESOL conference panel that gave rise to this collection (see the preface), I found myself looking back at books and articles I had read during my first year of graduate school. One of the articles, written by the late UCLA professor Clifford Prator, captures a sense of my own experience as a novice teacher. He writes:

> Conscientious teachers-to-be would presumably hope to find ... a coherent system of ideas, built up in an orderly fashion by the contributions of successive generations of authorities who made every effort to base their recommendations on experimental evidence and scientific fact. What they actually discover, if they sample the works on the subject written over the last fifty years, is something quite different. . . . At relatively brief intervals one highly touted "method" or "approach" has succeeded another in the favor of educators, and the proponents of each have tended to deny the validity of what preceded. (Prator, 1979, p. 5)

Prator explains by giving an example that other contributors to this collection can especially appreciate:

> The use of the mother tongue in the foreign language classroom has been successively emphasized, banned, required, and barely tolerated. (p. 5)

Prator then offers a metaphor to characterize the inconsistency he saw in the field:

> There have been similarly violent swings of the pendulum with regard to many other elements of language teaching. . . . Why does the pendulum swing so widely and rapidly from one extreme to another? Why have language teachers been able to achieve so little balance and continuity in their work? Is progress possible if it is continually necessary to begin over again? What reason is there to believe that currently approved methodology will last any longer than have its predecessors? In short in what is one to have faith, and why? (pp. 5–6)

My confessions here will illustrate some of the pendulum swings in my own beliefs and practices during the last 20-plus years. I offer this account as a cautionary tale for those who are now teachers in training, novice teachers, or even veterans in the interim state of complacency that Ilona Leki warns us about in her story. I have come to understand that teachers can and should resist pendulum swings if we have faith in our personal beliefs about language learning—beliefs based on research in our field and tempered by careful reflection of practice, our own and that of our colleagues.

A Novice's Approach to Blending Research and Practice

The first ESL class I ever taught was an advanced, multi-skills course with a curriculum in which writing held a central position. Early in the term, Liz Thornton, a more experienced teacher, arranged to observe my class. Because I was proud of my emerging familiarity with research, I turned to methods textbooks and then-current journal articles when planning the lesson she was to see. Although I've tried since then to eradicate the memory of that class, images still appear, like flashes of a nightmare.

Believing that transitional expressions were a key component of successful writing, to prepare for Liz's observation I consulted the first edition of *The Grammar Book,* by Marianne Celce-Murcia and Diane Larsen-Freeman (1983), a classic text now in its second edition (1999). In it, I found a chapter that draws on a study by Maureen Secord (1978), and I reviewed her findings. Influenced by the work of M. A. K. Halliday and R. Hasan (1976), Secord categorizes logical connectors according to semantic function: four main groups (additive, adversative, causal, and sequential), divided into more specific subcategories, each containing numerous logical connectors and labeled by their relative degree of formality and informality—easily more than 100 words and phrases. My task as a composition teacher seemed obvious: prepare a neat handout listing every transitional expression in the English language on one page, then review the handout with my students during the class session.

The day I think of as "transitional expression" day, Liz came to observe. I remember the crowded but comprehensive handout I had prepared for the students, the corresponding overhead transparency I projected on a screen, and the colored washable pens I used to highlight the categories. I can remember reciting the information, probably quite clearly and efficiently; I'm sure I didn't tarry, since we must have had other work to cover during the hour. But in my enthusiasm to plan and carry out the lesson, I missed this advice from Celce-Murcia and Larsen-Freeman (1983):

> The first time a new logical connector is presented to a class, it should be shown in a meaningful discourse context and also in the position in which it typically occurs in a sentence. (p. 329)

In the UCLA program, the practice was for a teacher and an observer to complete notes about a lesson separately and then meet later to discuss their notes. In comparing notes, Liz found lovely ways to compliment aspects of my class. But much more importantly, she found ways to begin a discussion about the teaching of writing, awakening me to the inherent advantages of contextualizing linguistic information, exploring prewriting activities, using student writing as authentic material, and integrating rhetorical modes. These many years later, I still appreciate that conversation and continue to draw on her advice. Initially, though, I was so embarrassed by my attempt to overload my students that I overreacted. Not only did I begin doubting my own beliefs and practices much too readily, but I vowed not to make such a foolish mistake again. The pendulum had swung.

Ignoring Utility

Not much later, I was to teach an advanced ESL composition course, which had previously been taught by three very experienced teachers: Frances Butler, Mary McGroarty, and Donna Brinton, colleagues at UCLA then. It was my good fortune that they were willing to share their course materials with me. In reviewing the materials, I noticed that they each used dictation as a regular classroom technique, reminding me of advice my first supervisor at UCLA, Bill Gaskill, had given me about the value of beginning every class with a short activity, one that students would expect and that could introduce the day's lesson. He mentioned a variety of possibilities, like a new vocabulary word or phrasal verb to record in a log, a joke, words of wisdom, a newspaper headline—in other words, a brief, regular, mini-lesson with linguistic and cultural benefits. I thought maybe a dictation exercise could serve that purpose.

Initially, I chose passages for dictation that appealed to me. I found that I liked the regularity of the task. I would read a passage to the students and then distribute a copy of the passage for them to see. Gradually, though, I began to see more potential benefits. I chose passages that were models of good writing and were related to the theme of our current unit. I saw that they also provided new vocabulary, grammatical structures, and punctuation choices to consider in context. Plus, knowing we would begin the day's lesson with a dictation, students began arriving in class on time, pulling paper and pen from notebooks to be ready for my first reading of the passage. They had a chance to hone their proofreading skills when the dictation was over and once again when they reviewed a classmate's paper by comparing it to the typed version of the text. And students became more engaged in discussions because the ideas in the passage served as a springboard for the day's lesson. Among the benefits students reported was that having to listen attentively and write quickly seemed to help them listen and take notes in large lecture courses.

This practice remained part of my repertoire until I taught in a different program. In the new context, instructors not only did not use dictation but looked on it with disfavor. Trying to blend in with my new colleagues, I quietly excluded it from my teaching. With this decision the pendulum had swung again. Similar to the way I had dropped transitional expressions from my repertoire, I dropped dictations, yet I didn't see the parallel. What I failed to do was consider my decision in light of students' positive evaluation of, and my own discoveries about, the practice's utility.

Oversubscribing to New Influences

Although I would like to claim that I became less vulnerable to pendulum swings of my own making, I didn't, in fact, for a long while. In the first years of my career, always with the best of intentions, I naively oversubscribed to new influences, choosing between what seemed like opposite and competing tensions. Rather than seeing the tensions as possibilities for making teaching and learning more complex, I felt drawn to choose one approach and abdicate another, very much like my experience with transitional expressions and dictations. Thus, I continued to construct false dichotomies: formulating a thesis statement versus discovering through writing; textbooks arranged by rhetorical modes versus theme-based texts; lengthy responses to my students' essays versus minimalist responses to avoid appropriation; writing conferences as minilectures versus virtual silence. I mistakenly saw them all as *either/or.*

One of the most significant false dichotomies I was attracted to was the product/process tension. About the time that most composition teachers around the U.S. were paying attention to the value placed on process, I began teaching in a writing program at the University of California, Berkeley. The program served both native and non-native speakers of English (as most American classrooms must). Since the architects of the program, the director, most of my new colleagues, and I were committed to a process approach, my classes became writing workshops. These workshops were almost exclusively student centered, with very little teacher talk occurring. In them, I emphasized the recursive nature of collaborative planning, invention strategies, drafting, peer response, and revising. And portfolios became the accepted, and often the only acceptable, form of assessment, since among process advocates, timed writing in particular was regarded as synonymous with gatekeeping—a punitive exercise, a stumbling block for writers, too reminiscent of in-class final exams that determined whether a student passed or failed the writing course.

For a while, I was satisfied to foster a community of writers in my classes, focus less on handouts and overhead transparencies, and overlook grammatical inaccuracies in deference to fluency and content. I rarely addressed rhetorical patterns or linguistic forms. And although I personally didn't regard in-class essays, short-answer quizzes, or other timed writing activities as punitive per se, I nevertheless lost sight of my belief that timed writing has important benefits and that assessment is a valuable part of teaching and learning. Once again, the pendulum had swung.

Reflecting and Learning from Others

Fortunately, I began to sense that my practice had swung too far. And luckily for me, the wisdom of colleagues was there for the taking. Clifford Prator was one such colleague, whose earlier influence had helped me reconsider the direction my teaching was taking. And once again, his advice gave me direction. I remembered a conversation with him about his observations of ESL writing classes at UCLA. Prator had said that he had seen no evidence that the specific needs of second language students were being addressed. He wondered if we could point to differences between the writing classes on campus that were being offered in programs for native-English-speaking students and those being offered for ESL students in the ESL program. Although I was now in a different context, I began to wonder the same thing, particularly about my own classes. What specialized knowledge from my graduate work (second language acquisition, contrastive analysis, error analysis, interlanguage analysis, testing, and linguistics) was I applying in my lessons? Decidedly not enough.

Although Liz's earlier observation of my class had presented me with a chance to move toward reflective teaching, it took me a long time to do that. I started to see that reflection could have prevented the pendulum swings that characterized my early years of teaching. Realizing that, I began to pay particular attention to conference presentations and published articles that I found to be immediately inspirational and applicable. For example, when Ann M. Johns (1990) shared insights about English for Academic Purposes, she reminded me that writing is indeed important in the university community. Lynn Goldstein and Susan Conrad (1990) described for me a way to include talk and silence in negotiating revision plans during writing conferences. Christine Holten and Jan Frodesen (1994) highlighted for me the importance of sentence-level grammar and discourse considerations to achieve rhetorical goals. Dana Ferris (1995) helped me focus on how students can understand cohesion and coherence by analyzing the structure of sentences to investigate the framework of topic and comment instead of subject and predicate. The work of these and other colleagues has informed and reassured me, helping me strike a better balance between change and continuity in my own teaching.

In addition to publications and conference presentations, ongoing conversations with colleagues have tempered
my approach to teaching. For example, when Terry Santos
(now teaching at Humboldt State University in California) and
I talk, the conversations inevitably linger with me, giving me a
different perspective to ponder, as she gave many people in
the field something to ponder in her widely cited article on
ideology (Santos, 1992). While teaching at UCLA together,
Terry and I had made different choices for our writing classes.
One such choice was her instruction on rhetorical patterns to
help students accomplish particular discourse functions; I
had all but abandoned this as too mechanical, allowing students instead to discover their own organizational schemes.
Her practice gave me pause, and talking with her about her
reasons for this choice led me to reconsider mine. As a consequence, I began to include overt explanations of these clas-
sical patterns. Although we no longer teach together, she and
I continue to compare perspectives on student populations
and writing programs, how those writers and programs might
call for different classroom approaches and institutional policies. Even when she listens to me talk about a single student,
our discussions encourage me to explore new issues, most
recently in the area of undiagnosed learning disabilities in
second language writers.

When I talk with Cherry Campbell (now at Sonoma State
University in California), I see how her work combines theory
and practice in ways Clifford Prator advocated. She models
this blend in her classes and in her own professional life. For
example, her research on writers' use of source material in
academic essays (1990) has found its way into her undergraduate composition classrooms—and into mine. Her
reflective teaching practices lead her to conferences where
she listens to speakers as carefully as she makes presentations to them. When Cherry periodically pauses to summarize
her teaching and research (see, e.g., Campbell, 1998), she

reinforces for me the value of reflecting on teaching, refining our teaching, and sharing insights with other teachers.

Barbara Kroll's invitation to participate on the panel at TESOL 1996 served exactly that same purpose for me. By reflecting on my experiences, I could identify the pendulum swings I've described here. Yes, I agree that a process-oriented writing class helps students develop identities as writers. Yes, I agree with the move in assessment toward direct testing and portfolio models. Yes, I agree that we lack empirical evidence to show that error identification or correction actually works. I find room, however, to return to kernels within my earliest beliefs and practices because I feel wary about dropping precisely what we ESL writing specialists can uniquely offer our students: linguistic training, quantitative and qualitative research skills, and a rich history of language teaching. I even find room in my current classes for dictations, in part because of a slim volume called *Dictation: New Methods, New Possibilities* (Davis & Rinvolucri, 1988). Its introduction describes the atmosphere in the authors' teacher-training workshops whenever they ask who uses dictation in their classes:

> At first only a few hands go up. There is inhibition in the air—can one admit to doing something as reprehensible and old-fashioned as dictation in what is meant to be a progressive, "communicative" workshop? What might colleagues think? (p. 1)

The book bolstered my confidence, prompting me to make a conference presentation about using this technique in a university composition classroom (Erickson, 1990)—a heretical notion to some. But by then I was more confident because I had examined the role of dictations in my classes, considered my students' evaluation of the technique, and found the endorsement by Davis and Rinvolucri validating.

Teachers would be wise to consider the answer Prator provides to his question, "In what is one to have faith, and why?" He reminds us:

> Language teaching must be both an art and a science. To the extent that it remains an art, it permits the individual teacher to exercise such personal gifts as s/he may be endowed with. To the extent that it can be related to a science or sciences and thus itself become an applied science, it can be developed in a coherent way, be given continuity, and be taught. The most successful teacher will always be something of an artist. But the art will be enhanced rather than destroyed if it is exercised within a framework of scientifically established guidelines. Therein lies the possibility of faith. (p. 6)

Prator's response remains timely. I not only agree with it but am inspired by this view of teaching. An additional element, however, comes from considering experiences like the ones I have described in this tale. I see that more than having the best of intentions, if I reflect on my own teaching as well as on the tales my colleagues tell, I am likely to change in reasonable ways and become less vulnerable to sweeping pendulum swings in the future.

References

Campbell, C. (1990). Writing with others' words: Using background reading text in academic compositions. In B. Kroll (Ed.), *Second language writing: Research insights for the classroom* (pp. 211–230). New York: Cambridge University Press.

Campbell, C. (1998). *Teaching second-language writing: Interacting with text.* Boston: Heinle & Heinle.

Celce-Murcia, M., & Larsen-Freeman, D. (1983). *The grammar book.* Rowley, MA: Newbury House Publishers.

Celce-Murcia, M., & Larsen-Freeman, D. (1999). *The grammar book* (2nd ed.) Boston: Heinle & Heinle.

Davis, P., & Rinvolucri, M. (1988). *Dictation: New methods, new possibilities.* Cambridge, UK: Cambridge University Press.

Erickson, M. (1990, November). A role for dictation in writing classes. Paper presented at the Northern Regional Conference of California Teachers of English to Speakers of Other Languages, San Francisco.

Ferris, D. R. (1995). Can advanced ESL students become effective self-editors? *CATESOL Journal, 8,* 41–62.

Goldstein, L. M., & Conrad, S. (1990). Student input and the negotiation of meaning in ESL writing conferences. *TESOL Quarterly, 24,* 443–460.

Halliday, M. A. K., & Hasan, R. (1976). *Cohesion in English.* London: Longman.

Holten, C., & Frodesen, J. (1994, March). Discourse perspectives on ESL errors in composition: Classroom and tutoring strategies for revision. Paper presented at the Conference on College Composition and Communication, Nashville, TN.

Johns, A. M. (1990). L1 composition theories: Implications for developing theories of L2 composition. In B. Kroll (Ed.), *Second Language writing: Research insights for the classroom* (pp. 24–36). New York: Cambridge University Press.

Prator, C. (1979). The cornerstones of method. In M. Celce-Murcia & L. McIntosh (Eds.), *Teaching English as a second or foreign language* (pp. 5–16). Rowley, MA: Newbury House Publishers.

Santos, T. (1992). Ideology in composition: L1 and ESL. *Journal of Second Language Writing, 1,* 1–15.

Secord, M. (1978). A categorization of transitional expressions in English. Unpublished master's thesis. UCLA.

Ilona Leki reflects on her life in this way. *Kaleidoscopes of accents and languages flash through my life. Various immediate family members speak or have studied in detail a dozen languages—German, Polish, Russian, English, French, Spanish, Nepali, Italian, Portuguese, Farsi, Arabic, Japanese. My best friend in elementary school spoke only Latvian at home; my third best friend, only Greek. Both these friends and others had trouble understanding my father's English; he accused them of listening with an "accent." My mother learned English from public television. I try to use these experiences to keep remembering how language both opens you up and shuts you down.*

Not the End of History

Ilona Leki
University of Tennessee

Like most of the voices in this volume, mine references a career as an L2 writing teacher that started some time ago and more or less grew out of experience with and interest in foreign language learning and teaching, not writing. My parents and I were bilingual before we immigrated to the U.S. Once here, my parents worked hard at learning their third language, English, in our (like Tony Silva's) multiethnic, working-class neighborhood, where hearing languages other than English was commonplace. Reflecting the ideology that is still current in much of this country, the immigrant children of the neighborhood did their best to minimize, if not hide, their multiethnicity and multilingualism in attempting to become indistinguishable from the native English speakers on television. Even now, in referring to my childhood environment, I cannot help but wonder how not having had English as a first language affects my professional credibility. Nevertheless, perhaps it was partly this background that made studying languages seem appealing and eventually led me to ESL.

By the time I began teaching ESL at the university level, I had a Ph.D. in French, graduate training in foreign language teaching, a fair amount of experience attempting to learn a variety of other languages, and experience teaching ESL abroad and in a community setting. Because of this background and in spite of the fact that I had no degree in TESL/applied linguistics, I felt I had some insight into what it took to learn another language. Perhaps I had even more understanding of the experiences of non-native-English-speaking students on campus than did my senior colleagues who were monolingual English speakers and who, to my astonishment, found it entirely untroubling that they were.

Without training or experience in teaching writing, I was hired to teach lower-level English language courses, not the more advanced and more prestigious writing courses my senior colleagues taught. Although I had never given much thought to teaching writing, and in fact disliked writing, found it difficult, and still do, it was clear that these writing courses were the real stuff, the serious stuff, and I aspired to being called upon to teach them some day. When that day came, I learned how (so I thought) by faithfully imitating my senior colleagues and faithfully following the textbook used in the program.

I started with very little of my own, but even if I had had a degree in TESL/applied linguistics, as Barbara Kroll and Linda Lonon Blanton note, at the time there were no special teacher-training classes devoted to teaching L2 writing or reading. Furthermore, I came out of high-school and freshman comp classes—whatever it was we did there—innocent even of the knowledge that English had some sort of describable way of organizing its writing that might be taught and learned. So following my leaders, when I first started teaching ESL writing, I did things like these.

- I asked students to write on incredibly bland and trivial subjects I myself certainly could not have written on with any kind of enthusiasm or interest whatsoever, like: *Compare three restaurants in town. In your essay be sure to include and underline the following structures: a participial phrase, a gerund, and an adjective clause.* Students got points off for not remembering to underline.

- I made students include a thesis statement in each essay and begin each paragraph with a topic sentence. This requirement was particularly ironic, if not ridiculous, since before teaching the writing course I really had never heard of thesis statements or topic sentences, although I figured they must be good things to include. They were in the textbook, after all. But I was actually learning about them at the same time my students were. And in exercises that directed students to select the most appropriate thesis statement/topic sentence, I was never sure myself what the correct answer was—and there was always only one correct answer.

- I taught rhetorical patterns and forced students to force their writing into them, so that the patterns themselves became obstacles instead of possibly facilitative frameworks.

- I tried to get students to write paragraphs consisting of a topic sentence, three examples, and a conclusion, as in the facetious essay prompt: *Describe the universe and give three examples.* I remember that one student thanked me heartily for giving him a writing formula he said he could now use in writing for all his classes.

- I had students read supposedly richly descriptive passages with all kinds of "strong verbs" and uncommon adjectives and then asked them to write a description of their own, imitating the one they had read.

- I marked every error on their papers—and of course these were on final drafts, since there were no other drafts—and made the students rewrite correctly every sentence where an error had appeared—rewrite the whole sentence. I figured it would be good for them.

- I gave top grades to error-free papers regardless of any-thing else in the papers because it was hard to justify not giving top grades to error-free papers.

I did a number of other naive and embarrassing things that I do not do now and would not recommend doing. I no longer think these are particularly good ways of helping students learn to write or even acquire spoken English. In my defense and in the defense of the people whom I was imitating and who were training me, the profession as a whole seemed to feel that teaching writing meant the teaching of grammatical and possibly rhetorical forms, a point noted by nearly everyone in this collection.

Then one fall during that time, I had an Iranian student who was taking my ESL freshman composition class as a senior, in fact as a *graduating* senior. Since this writing course was a requirement for graduation, if he failed it, he wouldn't graduate. True, he should have taken the course earlier to avoid finding himself in such a precarious position. I can only speculate why he postponed until he was a senior a course that would supposedly have helped him pass all his other courses, which obviously he was passing just fine, thank you, without the aid of having written on three restaurants in town and underlined selected grammatical structures. Despite succeeding in his other undergraduate "academic" courses, in my ESL writing course he was not doing very well, writing about those restaurants but probably forgetting to underline the grammatical structures.

By the end of the term, his passing or failing the course finally rode on his passing the final in-class, surprise-topic, one-shot essay, the type still used in many placement, proficiency, and exit exams around the country. And his essay was not very good. It was filled with grammatical errors, though it was not altogether devoid of life. Partly for that reason and partly because of the grave consequences for him of failing the course, I debated long and hard over whether or not to pass the paper, which meant pass him for the course and let him graduate. I even asked other teachers to read it to help me decide what to do.

I didn't pass the paper. Too many errors. About 10 P.M. that day, right after I finished figuring final grades, I left for Christmas vacation in Florida. I drove nonstop all night through Georgia, wide awake, fretting about what I had done. Something seemed to me very wrong about this whole way to teach writing.

A New Direction

After this traumatic experience (for me and no doubt for the student), I spent a great deal of time reading about teaching writing, and one of the first books I hit on was Ken Macrorie's (1970) book *Uptaught,* in which he coins the term "Engfish" to refer to the boring, bland, pointless writing that goes on in English writing classes for native speakers. He gives the example of an English teacher coming into the classroom on the day of the final exam, an in-class, one-shot essay, and putting on the board the writing prompt for the final essay: one word, "Bells." Reading about that actually made me feel a little better about the three restaurants.

After reading Macrorie and various writings by such key L1 researchers as Donald Murray, James Moffett, Peter Elbow, and Stephen Judy,[1] I was converted and transformed. Process was the answer. My pendulum, like Melinda Erickson's, began to swing. I started to let students choose their own topics, required multiple drafting, and orchestrated peer responding, all with the confidence that now I had finally found the way to teach writing. So at this time I did these things.

- I had students peer edit each other's papers, even though it was clear that they couldn't, that they missed obvious errors, and that they found errors where none existed, to the annoyance of the students who wrote the papers.

- I had students revise every paper they wrote, once for content, once for accuracy. They hated this routinized expenditure of time and effort.

- I covered their papers with responses to every idea they mentioned, including stray thoughts and suggestions as they occurred to me, to show how engaged I was as a real reader of their texts. They were overwhelmed.

- I expected them to show up in class with prewriting they had been assigned to do at home. If they came with a mere seven or eight phrases, I took that to show they had not done the work assigned. I thought that waiting until the last minute to write an assignment obviously meant not taking it seriously.

- I ran the class as a workshop and expected students to be able to compose in class. If they couldn't because they needed a different context, or coffee, or a radio on to help them think through their ideas, I was shocked to find some working not on their essays but on their math.

- I had them read and respond to the content of each other's papers and never looked at what they said.

- When they told me they did not know whether or not to follow the advice of a peer, I told them they were the authors and just had to decide for themselves whether or not to make recommended changes. Those decisions constituted their commitment to their writing, a way to make this writing their own, I told them.

- In a fit of egalitarianism I also wrote a "peer" response to their papers and expected them to treat mine as just one among several they collected from classmates.

Because I was excited about these techniques and because teaching was so central in my life, as I worked to juggle course materials or experimented with new techniques, I now believe I had an exaggerated view of how important this course was, or should have been, to students. When they told me that their engineering courses required no writing and were more important to them than English and asked why they had to waste time taking writing courses, I trotted out platitudes I had learned about how language (including writing) was the foundation of their education and that was why English—that is, *my* class—was probably the most important of their university careers.

I don't do or believe any of those things now either. Despite the many advantages and improvements that process approaches brought to teaching writing, I, along with Alister Cumming, no longer believe that there is a single, straightforward answer to helping writers improve or that rigidly sticking to the tenets of any particular teaching approach is appropriate. Also problematic, as Tony Silva puts it in a slightly different context, is looking for generalized answers to local questions. In my own case, I had been implementing techniques imported from first language writing and following the advice of L1 writing professionals.

Clearly, learning to write in L2 is *not* like learning to write in L1. Furthermore, despite the popularity of the metaphor, learning to write the language one already speaks is not the same as learning a second language. Presuming that learning to write in L1 is just like learning a second language trivializes the enormous effort it takes to learn a new language and then write extended prose in that language. And it demeans the enormous achievement of managing to do so. (See Matsuda & Jablonski, 1998, for a discussion of this issue.)

Like Melinda Erickson, I came to see the wisdom of these questions: How are L2 classes different from L1 classes? And what specific knowledge is necessary to teach them? When L2 students asked for examples/models of the writing they were being asked to produce, or when they claimed that part of what held them back in writing was lack of vocabulary, it seemed it was time to listen to them and not to first language writing researchers.

One of my most precious enlightenments at the time came, however, after I began to notice something odd and bewildering about L2 writers. First, like my Iranian student described earlier, students who were not doing particularly well in my writing class seemed to be doing fine in many of their other courses at the university. Second, in the writing they were doing in other courses, they seemed to be grappling with much more sophisticated ideas than they addressed in my class. And most confusing, students in the third semester of our writing courses who had gone through the first two semesters did not do as well as students who placed directly into the third course.

The key to these puzzles was a realization that dawned on me slowly but that was profoundly liberating: My students would not learn to write in English once and for all *in my class.* Learning language and learning to write take time and effort. My classes could help them with some aspects of their task, could provide some positive experiences with writing, but their long-term success in writing was not about my teaching and not about my class. It is always about *their* lives and learning. And their learning, including learning language and learning to write, will take place in a variety of settings, not just in my class, and over time, not just in the two or three semesters institutionally designated as sufficient.

I wish I had known in some deep way long ago that it is not the curriculum or the pedagogy or the textbook or me but the students themselves who are the central players in this drama. As Melinda Erickson and Alister Cumming point out, teaching is simply not as important as learning. My students did not come to my class as blank slates, as Linda Lonon Blanton puts it. I did not have to teach them everything in my class, and they did not have to learn, and in fact could not learn, everything in my class.

Still Not There

But just so my story does not sound like "once I was lost but now I'm saved," I need to go on. Just a couple of years ago I was teaching an experimental special writing class for graduate students and found myself again in the midst of following a principle that I finally realized made sense as a principle but was ineffective in the context in which I was applying it. In the class I wanted students to be writing about topics related to their majors and *not* wasting time writing about customs or holidays in their countries, but I was also working to get across the idea that writers need to be sensitive to audience needs. The audience for these students was to be the rest of the class and me. In peer-responding sessions, we would be reading each other's writing. In order to understand that writing, coming, as it was, from a variety of disciplinary areas, it had to be in nontechnical terms.

At first I ignored students' complaints that it was difficult for them to write in nontechnical terms for a nonspecialist audience. Sure it's hard, I said. It's always hard to take the audience into account. Keep trying. It took me a while, but I finally got it into my head that not only was I asking these students to write in a foreign language but that I also wanted them to translate the English they knew, their disciplinary English, into general-audience English instead of allowing them to write the technical English they were reading and using in classes in their disciplines. It was as though I was gratuitously asking them to use yet another foreign language.

I think part of my problem in all these situations has to do with experiencing a kind of complacency I have come to fear, which may in a certain way be endemic to our ESL profession, especially for those of us who have spoken, read, and written English more or less all our lives. We get used to always being right, infallible even, in relation to learners of English, and this cocky sense of being right puts our critical capacities to sleep. For years we have talked in the professional literature about wanting our students to think critically, as if they didn't and couldn't do so without our intervention in their development.

Anyone who thinks international university students, regardless of their cultural backgrounds, cannot think critically about elements of their lives *that they know something about* has not talked to them enough. Just ask what they think of the TOEFL, or the university's English placement exams, or course requirements—or the ESL class they're taking, for that matter. The arrogance of this very assumption makes me sometimes wonder how much we ourselves think critically about what we do and what we assume.

The Critical Slope

I was just lately reminded again of how easy it is to slip into uncritical thinking. My recent research focuses on students' experiences writing across the curriculum because I was interested in learning what will be expected of them in classes outside of English. I hope with this information to organize our L2 English classes to be more beneficial to students in reading and writing for other classes. For example, I know that in courses across the curriculum, there is a great deal of reading assigned and that keeping up with the reading is often difficult for bilingual students at the university level. One response would be to try to change students so that they will be better equipped to accommodate institutional demands. So I might try to come up with ways to teach students to read faster to meet their professors' expectations, all the tricks like skimming, reading subtitles, and looking at (the infamous) topic sentences.

A different response, however, born of a more critical attitude, would lead me to think instead about questioning the requirement to read that much and that fast, to encourage students not just to accept but to question and, when necessary, to resist when excessive or inappropriate demands are placed on them. Otherwise, the message I communicate to them is that if they fail, if they cannot keep up with the reading, or if, for example, they cannot write a response to an essay question in the same amount of exam time allotted to their native-English-speaking peers, it's their own fault—they don't read fast enough, their English isn't good enough, they aren't fluent enough—rather than the fault of a system and of institutions that refuse to really accommodate diversity. These institutions are of course happy enough to trot out ESL students and their native costumes, foods, and folk dances in a display of the institutions' self-congratulatory commitment to multiculturalism.

The realization of the dangers of complacency and of the failure to critique my own assumptions has led me toward the hope of better developing and employing a consistently critical attitude toward the work I do. In line with this struggle, another change in the last few years has involved a shift in my view of the social aspects of teaching bilingual learners. For a number of reasons, centrally involving the marginalized status of many ESL programs and teachers in those programs, particularly teachers with part-time employment, some L2 writing professionals have followed the lead of L1 writing professionals in resisting the idea that writing courses are essentially service courses in the academy, as distinct from disciplinary courses. I understand, sympathize with, and have, for the sake of academic politics, publicly supported the argument that L2 writing courses are not service courses. But, in fact, I have always thought of my work as a form of service, though service to students rather than to any institution. I think of it as advocacy, almost as a form of social work.

A Broader Social Vision

What I have come to realize, however, through reading various works by such researchers and theorists as Alastair Pennycook, Sarah Benesch, Brian Morgan, Suresh Canagarajah, Bonny Norton Peirce[2] and others interested in critical pedagogy, is that my view of the social was excessively narrow, focused primarily on a fair deal for students within the context of their studies in the U.S. I believe now, however, that teachers are in a position to aim not just at the welfare of individual students but, in their role as cultural workers and through their students (Pennycook, 1996), at issues of social justice more generally.

We live with our students not only in the world of the university but also in the world. We can choose to make use of our knowledge and promote students' developing literacy either narrowly for personal advancement or more broadly to combat social injustice in our shared world. Reflective awareness of the world and of the import of our decisions in it is at the core of these choices. If making such writing assignments as comparing three restaurants results in boring, bland, pointless writing-as-exercise, it is also questionable from a more political point of view as, at the very least, a wasted opportunity.

Over the years, in the classroom and through my students, I know I have learned a great deal, though it pains me to think how much of this learning was on-the-job training and occasionally at the expense of others. I have learned that in second language writing we cannot let first language writing researchers do our thinking for us. I have learned that we cannot ignore students' expressed needs, wishes, and opinions about their learning because we are so sure we know better. I see that we need to develop and maintain respect for the complexity of what our students are about. I believe that as teachers we have social obligations to work toward improving the world we live in.

These are some of the morals of my story up to now. But in order to move beyond any given "now," I would argue that what goes on in the writing class or in any educational setting needs to be continuously informed by each of following:

- the research literature in L1 and L2—in order to find out what others are doing and thinking;
- our students—in order to respect their sense of what they hope for from a class; and
- our own felt sense of what is effective and appropriate for each of our classes—informed by constant reflection on, even fretting about, what we do so that we don't become complacent and so that we remember that thinking critically is not just for students.

For me it is important to repeatedly remind myself that our epoch is not the end of history. We need to keep listening to students and each other with open minds and to examine critically, constantly, what it is we do with students and ask them to do. The effects on their lives are dramatic and sometimes traumatic. While the theme of this collection is in some sense all that we did *not* know about teaching second language writing earlier in our careers, as a profession, as humans, our continuous, ongoing, relentless struggle also needs to be against thinking, "Now we know."

Notes

1. See, for example, Elbow (1981), Judy (1980), Moffett (1968), and Murray (1968).

2. Major publications by these theorists include the following: Benesch (1994, 2001), Canagarajah (1993a, 1993b), Pennycook (1996, 1998), Morgan (1992/93, 1998), and Norton Peirce (1989, 1995).

References

Benesch, S. (1994). ESL, ideology, and the politics of pragmatics. *TESOL Quarterly, 27,* 705–716.

Benesch, S. (2001). *Critical English for academic purposes: Theory, politics, and practice.* Mahwah, NJ: Erlbaum.

Canagarajah, S. (1993a). Critical ethnography of a Sri Lankan classroom: Ambiguities in opposition to reproduction through TESOL. *TESOL Quarterly, 27,* 601 626.

Canagarajah, S. (1993b). Up the garden path: Second language writing approaches, local knowledge, and pluralism. *TESOL Quarterly, 27,* 301–306.

Elbow, P. (1981). *Writing without teachers.* New York: Oxford University Press.

Judy, S. (1980). The experiential approach: Inner worlds to outer worlds. In T. Donovan & B. McClelland (Eds.), *Eight approaches to teaching composition* (pp. 37–52). Urbana, IL: National Council of Teachers of English.

Macrorie, K. (1970). *Uptaught.* New York: Hayden Book Company.

Matsuda, P., & Jablonski, J. (1998). Beyond the L2 metaphor: Toward a mutually transformative model of ESL/WAC collaboration. Available at <http://aw.colostate.edu/articles/matsuda_jablonski2000.htm>.

Moffett, J. (1968). *Teaching the universe of discourse.* Boston: Houghton Mifflin.

Morgan, B. (1992/93). Teaching the Gulf War in an ESL classroom. *TESOL Journal, 2 (2),* 13–17.

Morgan, B. (1998). *The ESL classroom: Teaching, critical practice, and community development.* Toronto: University of Toronto Press.

Murray, D. (1968). *A writer teaches writing: A practical method of teaching composition.* Boston: Houghton Mifflin.

Norton Peirce, B. (1989). Towards a pedagogy of possibility in teaching of English internationally. *TESOL Quarterly, 23,* 401–420.

Norton Peirce, B. (1995). Social identity, investment, and language learning. *TESOL Quarterly, 29,* 9–31.

Pennycook, A. (1996). Borrowing others' words: Text, ownership, memory, and plagiarism. *TESOL Quarterly, 30,* 201–230.

Pennycook, A. (1998). *The cultural politics of English as an international language.* New York: Longman.

Shaughnessy, M. (1977). *Errors and expectations.* New York: Oxford University Press.

Tony Silva, a fervent believer in ceaseless self-promotion, asks readers who are interested in learning more about theory, research, and practice in second language writing to consider reading and submitting manuscripts to the Journal of Second Language Writing *<http://www.jslw.org/>, attending and participating in the Symposium on Second Language Writing, and/or pursuing a master's or Ph.D. focused on second language writing at Purdue University.*

From the Working Class to the Writing Class
A Second-Generation American Teaches Second Language Composition

Tony Silva
Purdue University

At age 18, had I been informed by a fortune teller that in 30 years I would be a college professor spending most of my time thinking, reading, and writing about second language writing, I would have asked for my money back. To explain, I'll tell a story about my experience with language(s) and literacy, and, as tradition dictates, I'll follow that story with a moral—in the form of a brief sermon. First, the (making of a) teacher, then the (exhortations of a) preacher.

Beginnings of My Story

I was born in Bethlehem, Pennsylvania—a steel town at the time (the Bethlehem Steel Plant is now the Bethlehem Steel Museum)—to working-class parents, both first-generation Americans. My father was, indeed, a steelworker at that time; my mother, a homemaker. My mother had completed high school; my father had not. While my mother and father certainly had lasting influences on me, it was my grandparents who I think had a direct influence on why I do what I do now.

My father's parents were immigrants from Portugal. They never learned to speak English—my father, who could speak and understand Portuguese well enough, was the mediator in my communication with them. To the best of my knowledge, neither my grandfather (another steelworker) nor my grandmother (a homemaker) could read or write in English, and I suspect they could not do so in Portuguese either.

My mother's parents had immigrated from France (my grandmother) and Italy (my grandfather). They spoke more English than my father's folks, but not by much—I was able to communicate orally with them (with some difficulty) without a translator. My grandmother (a homemaker) could read and write some in English; my grandfather (a baker and, later on, a custodial worker for the city of Bethlehem) could not.

You might be thinking that in such a rich linguistic context, I grew up bilingual, or even tri- or quadrilingual. I did not. The (implicit) message that I got from my grandparents (usually via my parents) was that they had left "the old country" for good reason (basically, lack of economic opportunity) and were determined that their children and their children's children should make good in this foreign land. Their experience told them that the key to success was speaking (as well as reading and writing) English—and *only* English. My parents (mostly, my father) added a college education as a requirement for success. Thus, almost all of my foreign language learning (primarily in Spanish) took place in classrooms, not in my home or with my family.

I can't say that I really minded all this at the time—growing up with one language was enough for me—but now I do feel a bit miffed about having been limited to English. I think this accounts for my interest in those who are willing to go to strange and far-away places (like the USA can be for many) and learn not only to speak a new language (like English) but also to write it with distinction. I think this accounts for my choice to do what I do.

Biding Time

So back to my story. I spent my primary school years at Central School (not a pseudonym) on the south side of Bethlehem. To the extent that I remember, my experiences there were as nondescript as the school's name. I studied no foreign language (none was offered) and can only remember one writing assignment—a perfunctory report on Abraham Lincoln. I learned my readin', 'ritin', and 'rithmetic well enough, got good grades, and stayed out of trouble.

However, in my years at Central I was exposed to a very ethnically diverse group of people (students and teachers), but at the time—coming from a multiethnic family—I didn't find this remarkable. I also found that I liked to read and spent the days inhospitable to play (too hot, too cold, too wet) at the local public library, reading widely but randomly. I'm uncertain about the ramifications of this. What I now believe about the relationship between reading and writing makes me want to speculate that it kept any developing writing ability I might have had then from atrophying during my K–12 school years, since I can't recall doing much writing at all. On the other hand, when I began to write in college, it seemed like I was starting from scratch, and I don't remember feeling very comfortable with or confident about my writing until graduate school.

Junior high was much the same, except for the fact that in ninth grade students were given the opportunity to enroll in a course that I can best describe as a foreign language sampler. This year-long course was split into three parts—a third of the year each for Spanish, French, and German (no Portuguese or Italian, unfortunately). I can't say I learned a lot in this course—we focused primarily on learning numbers, days of the week, and that kind of stuff, with an occasional poem or song thrown in now and then. However, this course did pique or, perhaps better, *reinforce* my interest in foreign languages.

High school, though a social success, was an intellectual low point. I started high school in 1968 when the USA seemed to be melting down: assassinations, riots, protest marches, drugs, sex, and rock and roll—it was, to say the least, very stimulating. Who could get interested in learning about geometry or British literature with stuff like that going on? I turned on and tuned in but didn't drop out, because high school, after all, was a good place to meet people and because I didn't like the other option: working full-time at some miserable job—which I was already doing part-time. So for three years I counted the number of days I had until graduation and did my best to miss as many days as possible and to do as little work as I could on the days I did show up. I was rewarded for my efforts with a 2.4 (out of 4.0) high-school grade-point average. In retrospect, I think my teachers were generous.

Turning On to Languages

After graduation and after working at some of those miserable jobs I feared, I decided to go back to school. In spite of my dismal GPA, I was accepted (they needed warm bodies, I guess) at West Chester State College (in Pennsylvania) but just wasn't ready and dropped out before the end of the first semester. However, I do remember writing a paper on Led Zeppelin (laudatory, of course) for my English composition class. The instructor gave me an A and wrote something like "interesting" or "nice job" on my paper. I was pumped. I went to see him after class to ask him what in particular he liked. I got no details. He just said something like, "It's okay, but nothing to write home about." I wasn't discouraged. I liked what I'd written, too, and realized that, for me, the key to writing well was to write about something I knew and cared about.

I decided to go back home and give Northampton County Area Community College (NCACC) a try. This I was ready, even eager, for. Here I took, among other things, two composition classes. In one I remember the instructor playing Allman Brothers records while we wrote in class. The other instructor took a group of students (myself not included) to see *Deep Throat* (hey, this was the early 1970s) as a stimulus for discussion (it certainly was) and, ultimately, writing. There were possibilities here. Also, at NCACC, I got back into foreign languages. I hit it off well with my Spanish teacher and wound up taking all the Spanish courses the school offered and tutoring students in first- and second-semester Spanish. Having run out of Spanish courses to take, I dabbled in French. I was hooked.

Next stop: Kutztown State College (KSC, now Kutztown State University), where I majored in Spanish and did minors in French and English. Because I had done most of my required first- and second-year courses at NCACC, I was able to focus almost exclusively on language: American literature and English linguistics, some basic French, and lots of courses in Spanish—divided fairly evenly between literature and language.

It was in Spanish that I got my first appreciation of how difficult it was to read and write in a foreign language. With bilingual dictionary in hand, it took me a good two to three hours to read a 10-page short story. Writing essay exams and research papers in Spanish was even more challenging. I kept things short and walked the fine line between paraphrase and plagiarism. My instructors were kind; I got encouragement, support, and good grades. And, as at NCACC, I tutored students in first-year Spanish courses. I was at best, however, an intermediate-level Spanish learner, much less proficient in my L2 than are the undergraduate ESL writers I now teach.

Discovering ESL

After graduating from KSC, it didn't take long to see that no one wanted to hire me to explain the difference between *ser* and *estar* or discuss Cervantes. That is, language study was fun but not exactly lucrative: I worked off and on as a bartender, a hospital custodian, and as a claims taker for the Pennsylvania Office of Unemployment Compensation in Allentown (yes, the place Billy Joel sang about). This was not where I wanted to be.

Being often in between jobs, with time on my hands, I learned about a church-sponsored group that needed volunteers to tutor recent immigrants in English, and I eagerly signed up. Having come from immigrants, I wanted to get back to working with language. It was a wonderful experience. Though I really didn't know what I was doing, I was having fun and (I hope) helping people out.

At some later point, I learned that what I was doing for free could be done for a living, and I looked into and applied to a number of master's TESL programs. I was accepted at Southern Illinois University and the University of Illinois at Urbana-Champaign (UIUC). Not knowing how to judge such programs, I made the pragmatic move, choosing UIUC because they paid their teaching assistants more. I headed (mid)West.

Forays into Writingland

This turned out to be a smart move. At UIUC, I was teaching ESL at the Intensive English Institute (IEI) for Becky Dixon; taking courses from people like Doug Brown, Lyle Bachman, Sandra Savignon, and Braj Kachru (all major figures in the growing field of applied linguistics); and interacting with bright and interesting people from all over the world. I was getting paid more than the minimum wage to do all this. My two-year program ended way too soon.

Because I'd enjoyed the master's program at UIUC so much, I stuck around for a while, toying with the idea of continuing for a Ph.D. (but in what?). During this time I took a few classes and taught basic writing in the English Department's Educational Opportunity Program—my first experience in teaching writing. The course was current-traditional in approach (concerned primarily with the analysis of formal features of written texts—especially essays and term papers—and focused on the modes of discourse, usage, and style) and comprised of minority students, student athletes, and even ESL students, which made for interesting classroom dynamics.

I found it challenging to try to address students' common and individual needs but rewarding in that the class did coalesce and made (from my perspective) some progress— though I might be romanticizing here. As a writing teacher, I was textbook bound; that is, I planned my course according to what was in the prescribed textbook and did what the textbook told me to do. In retrospect, I believe I did this simply because I didn't know all that much about theories of writing and writing instruction. The textbook's author seemed to know more than I did, so I followed orders. My students and I were learning about writing from the book, not unlike what Barbara Kroll reports in her tale.

I was still textbook bound when I worked in the summer of 1982 at Harvard University's summer ESL program. Among the courses I taught was an elective course on commercial correspondence. I found a book on business-letter writing developed expressly for use with ESL writers and followed it faithfully. While I learned a lot from the book, after a week or so I realized that my students knew much more about business writing than I did. They were polite and humored me. My faith in basing a course on a book was shaken.

Throwing Out the Book

That fall, I returned to the IEI at UIUC as a full-time teaching associate (instructor and supervisor). Here I was put in charge of the writing component. Still not having a coherent understanding of writing and writing pedagogy, I was quite nervous about taking on this role. Things were different now because I not only had to teach writing but also had to develop curricula, choose textbooks, and supervise TAs.

At the beginning, I stuck with my "by the book" strategy, which worked out okay in some cases and not so well in others. I found the books I chose for beginning and low-intermediate writing classes to be teacher-friendly (for me and, as far as I could tell, for the TAs I was supervising). The students, I believe, found them useful and learned from them. What else could one hope for in a textbook? These books could be classified as taking a pattern-model approach. They focused on grammar, organization, and text types. Lessons typically included an introductory reading; exercises on comprehension, grammar, and vocabulary; a model text; and instructions for developing a composition based on the model text. I had similar results with the textbook I chose for high-intermediates. This book was cut from the same cloth but focused most of its attention on developing unified and coherent paragraphs and extrapolating paragraph principles to essays.

But there were problems at the advanced level. I tried a number of books (structural, functional, and whatever) that were hot off the press, but I wasn't satisfied. I felt that my students did not find them sufficiently challenging or interesting. Writing at this level seemed to be different in kind from writing at lower proficiency levels. In retrospect, I believe that two things caused me this discomfort: I enjoyed teaching at this level more than at the lower levels and thus was more invested in my work; and I was becoming more knowledgeable about and experienced in teaching writing. I didn't want to follow someone else's lead.

Thus began my serious disenchantment with using other people's materials and my efforts to develop my own, though unlike Joy Reid and Linda Lonon Blanton, who eventually did turn their materials into textbooks, I never did. I didn't realize how difficult writing one's own materials could be. An illustration of this was my experience in developing a curriculum for advanced students. It seemed to me that most of these students would very soon find themselves in non-ESL classes where they would need to complete academic writing assignments—particularly research papers of one type or another. I latched on to an assignment developed by colleagues from the English Department and the library for use with native-English-speaking, first-year writers. I thought of it as a controlled research paper—controlled in the sense that the teacher chose the topic and provided the texts (primarily articles from periodicals). The students were to take it from there.

I tried this assignment with a number of "science-y" topics, for example, gasohol—the use of ethanol in gasoline. While I was quite interested in exploring these topics, the students typically were not. In addition, the provided texts seemed too difficult for them. Undaunted, I researched and gathered material on a topic that could not miss—international students in the USA. It missed. It then dawned on me that I was doing the same thing as the writers whose textbooks didn't work for me: imposing on students a topic or theme that I found interesting and expecting them to share my enthusiasm for the enterprise.

I decided that if I wanted to keep on teaching composition, I would need to learn something about it. Being a good academic, I went to the library. I had heard the term *composi-*

tion used in conjunction with rhetoric, so I looked up *rhetoric* in the card catalogue. The first thing that turned up was Aristotle's "Rhetoric." I checked it out immediately and read it at one sitting. A bit dated, I thought, but very accessible and potentially useful. I was impressed with Aristotle's clarity, concision, and tone of certainty—things that I needed at that point in my life/career. Thus began my serious inquiry into rhetoric and composition.

My three-year contract at the IEI having run out, I followed my then–significant other and now-wife, Margie Berns, who had just completed her Ph.D. in linguistics, to the University of Florida, where she was offered a one-year visiting assistant professorship. I was pretty much just along for the ride, a faculty spouse (to be). I took some linguistics courses and taught an advanced reading and writing course in the university's intensive English program. Seeing myself as demoted from supervisor to teacher, not liking it, and consequently getting pretty cranky, I rejected the textbook that the program's director had chosen for my class and ordered a new one, which, again, I grew to dislike.

My "by the book" strategy was now bankrupt and had to go. It was at this point that I decided to seriously engage with the literature on L2 writing. I spent a lot of time at the university's library finding, photocopying, and closely reading anything about L2 writing I could find, something that I continue to do 15 years later, even as the quantity of available publications in the field has continued to expand exponentially.

Getting Serious about ESL Writing

In the spring of that year, Margie applied for and got a tenure-track job in the English Department at Purdue University. So at the end of the term, we packed up and headed north to West Lafayette, Indiana. She would be the director of ESL. I would again be a faculty spouse and perhaps a Ph.D.

student. At this time I didn't realize what a stroke of luck this was for me. I had not known that Purdue had a program in rhetoric and composition with a high national profile. Opportunity had knocked once again. I eagerly answered the door.

So I again joined the graduate-student ranks, pursuing a double major: linguistics, and rhetoric and composition. All incoming graduate students were required to teach the first-year writing sequence and were mentored while doing this. Even though I was required to use a book (a new type of book for me, one that had a familiar focus on texts but also paid serious attention to composing processes) and had to teach two sections of first-year writing, each enrolling about 25 students each semester (that's 50 papers to respond to every two weeks, on top of the work I was doing in my graduate courses), this was truly a learning and growth experience for me. It also reinforced my suspicion that there were salient differences between teaching first and second language writing.

In the graduate program, I got to take courses from prominent composition scholars like Janice Lauer, Jim Berlin, Patricia Sullivan, and Irwin Weiser. And at Purdue seminars and lectures, I was able to hear and see up close figures like Linda Flower, James Kinneavy, and Sharon Crowley, major figures in the growing field of composition studies. I was studying my old friend Aristotle, as well as Plato, Cicero, and Quintilian, and reading the work of state-of-the-art moderns (and even some post-moderns). I was swimming in mainstream composition studies but also pondering what all of this meant for L2 writing and writing instruction. It became evident to me that L2 writers were not on the mainstream's sonar screen, nor were mainstream writing scholars much interested in widening their scope to include L2 writing—they had enough on their plates already. I surmised that I and others interested in learning about and teaching second language writing were going to be pretty much on our own.

After my first year and throughout the rest of my time as

a student at Purdue, I taught second language writing classes (for undergraduate and graduate students). Disenchanted by L2 writing textbooks and not all that impressed with their L1 counterparts, I finally began to wean myself from using textbooks (though I was still willing to "borrow" heavily elements that I found useful in them). My attitude toward textbooks then and now is that most probably work exceedingly well for the author's students and in the author's institutional context but that they don't travel well; that is, contexts for teaching composition vary so greatly that the prospects of developing a textbook that is truly suitable for a mass (student or teacher) market are not good, regardless of what textbook publishers say (and with all due respect to my textbook-publishing colleagues represented in this volume).

I felt and continue to feel that L2 composition materials need to be local, not global. I set out to get to know my students (and their interests, perceived needs, and institutional contexts) better and to employ what I know about L1 and L2 writing in a program and in procedures designed specifically for them. To facilitate this I moved from topic-based writing (e.g., write a paper on Jimi Hendrix) to task-based writing (e.g., write a profile of someone you admire) and tried to integrate what I saw to be the best features of the text-based (e.g., paying attention to text structure and the appropriate use of language) and process-based traditions (e.g., suggesting strategies for planning, writing, and revising). By the time I finished my Ph.D. program at Purdue, I felt that I had achieved some modest success in this enterprise.

During my last year at Purdue, I accepted a job at Auburn University, there being no opening at Purdue. I spent a very interesting and enjoyable year as the director of ESL at Auburn, but I didn't do much with regard to writing that year, except for building the foundations for the *Journal of Second Language Writing,* which Ilona Leki and I still edit today.

Developing Curriculum

Opportunity knocked yet again: A tenure-track job in ESL at Purdue became available, and I was lucky enough to get it. Soon I was heading back to West Lafayette and to Margie. Here, I was to direct the ESL writing program, mentor TAs teaching in the program, and teach (mostly) graduate courses in ESL, including a seminar on second language writing. I would also be a member of both the English language and linguistics, and rhetoric and composition programs. It couldn't get much better than this.

I found myself in charge of developing and supervising four writing courses for ESL students: three at the undergraduate level and one at the graduate level. Despite my prior negative experiences with textbooks, I spent a couple of years trying out different ESL writing textbooks for these courses, to no avail. (I have no idea of the cause of this relapse.) Finally, I realized that I needed to design and develop my own curricula. Luckily for me, Ilona Leki had just published an article about sequencing writing assignments (Leki, 1991/92), providing me with a course description that fit the bill for a freshman-level writing course.

In the plan, students choose their own topic for the semester and look at it from several different angles—writing what they know about it and their personal investment in it, summarizing articles on the topic, doing a survey on it, interviewing an expert about it, and putting it all together in an expository or argumentative essay. Topics chosen are, for example, autism (by a student who had cared for an autistic younger brother) and the human cost of earthquakes (by a student who had experienced a particularly devastating one). This approach clicked for me and to a great extent solved my "textbook problem."

The second-semester course for freshmen was (still is) a tougher nut to crack. What I finally did was to make it parallel to the first-semester course, moving from topics of personal interest to topics of academic interest (still chosen by students). The writing assignments—a paper on students' knowledge of and motivation for writing about their topic, a research-paper proposal, an annotated bibliography, a literature review—culminate in a library (now, largely, a Web-based) research paper. In the course, students opt for topics such as the effect of international politics on tourism (from a student in hotel and restaurant management) or the protection of coral reefs (from a student in environmental studies).

As a result of these changes, both of these first-year courses began to go very smoothly. There was, however, one big problem: each course enrolled 24 to 25 students—a number much too large, in my view, for a truly successful advanced ESL writing class. This over-enrollment in ESL writing (and in mainstream classes as well) still plagues me to the extent that I've come to feel that it's the single most significant impediment to quality writing instruction.

The course for international graduate students was a different matter altogether. What I inherited was a six-hour non-credit course with no obvious focus or purpose, at least not that I could discern. This was problematic: imagine how it would feel to be required to take a six-hour course for no credit, in addition to a nine- to twelve-hour course load in one's major. Needless to say, the course was a hard sell. Trying to make some sense out of it, I was able to strike a deal with my department head—the six-hour course with a 15-student limit would become a three-hour course with a 10-student limit: less expense for the department; smaller classes for teachers—a win-win situation. It's still noncredit, though, but I'm working on that.

Developing a curriculum for this graduate course was also a challenge because its population included students at a number of different levels (from first-year master's students to doctoral students in their last semester) and from a wide range of disciplines (but mostly science and technology). The question was how to develop a curriculum that made sense for such a diverse group of students. My answer has been to develop assignments that I hope are of common interest and use for all involved—for example, a writer's autobiography, a resume, a conference proposal, a research-grant proposal, a manuscript review/critique. This allows for a situation in which the assignments are task based, similar to how the two-semester sequence at the undergraduate level is designed. Another thing I tried with the graduate course was to do it as a tutorial. That is, the teacher would meet with each student individually for an hour each week to work on writing assignments for their non-composition courses. Sounds optimal, right? Wrong. The problem was that many of the students had no or very few writing assignments in their other courses. I let this plan expire quietly, perhaps another example of how the best of intentions, as Melinda Erickson puts it in her tale, don't always pan out.

This brings to an end the account of my experiences as an L2 writing teacher. At this point, I want to acknowledge that whatever good I've managed to do has been greatly facilitated by others—I get by with a lot of help from my friends, colleagues, and students. I have tried to give something back in the form of my work with the *Journal of Second Language Writing* and the Symposium on Second Language Writing and my service to the professional organization TESOL and to the Conference on College Composition and Communication (CCCC).

Preaching a Sermon

I'd like to end with some unsolicited advice for novice ESL writing teachers, followed by a brief description of the principles that guide my work in L2 writing. (Keep in mind that what I say primarily reflects my experience with advanced L2 writers in institutions of higher learning in the USA.)

I have come to see writing as an extremely complex and fascinating process—perhaps the most complex thing that a human being can do. And doing it in a second language adds another layer of complexity. I also believe that research on writing (especially basic research on writing, as opposed to research on writing instruction) has barely scratched the surface of this amazing phenomenon. I know that I now feel much less knowledgeable about writing than I did when I started teaching.

In my view, teaching writing (L1 or L2) requires at least three things: knowledge, experience, and flexibility or open-mindedness, each of which is necessary but not sufficient for successful writing instruction. Knowledge is worth nothing if it is dogmatic and untempered by ongoing experience. Decades in the writing classroom are no advantage for teachers who do not stay abreast of developments or reflect on what goes on in their classes. And neither flexibility nor open-mindedness will be of help to writing instructors without some explicit understanding of writing and without hands-on experience in the classroom. So, as you might expect, I try to keep up with the professional literature, make sure I teach writing on a regular basis, and do my best to maintain an open mind and flexible position.

Here's where I am today (but maybe not tomorrow). I am committed to a pedagogy that, at the very least, seriously takes into consideration the strategic, rhetorical, and textual dimensions of writing—that is, composing processes, relations between the reader and writer, and the formal and functional features of texts, as well as the contexts (institutional, societal, political, and ideological) in which instruction takes place (cf. Ann M. Johns's chapter in this volume, which discusses some of these critical factors from a somewhat different angle). Let me explain how this plays out in my teaching.

On students and their writing processes: I believe that the better I know my students and understand their composing processes and perceptions about writing and writing instruction, the more effective I can be in helping them build their confidence and competence in writing in English. I attempt to identify and work from where my students are, not from where I want or expect them to be. My teaching is structured around what I see as the basic elements of composing processes: planning, writing, and revising.

These days, I am more interested in learning about and nurturing the (successful) planning strategies my students are already using than in conducting elaborate off-the-shelf planning activities. I ask students to write (at home, not under time pressure in the classroom) multiple drafts—at least three—and I respond to each, preferably in one-to-one conferences.

Recent research and my own experience have led me to largely eschew peer response. I can't disagree with students who feel (justifiably, in my view) that they get better feedback from their teacher than from their peers—especially in regard to linguistic matters. I typically address matters of content and text structure in the first draft and linguistic and mechanical issues in the second and provide learners with both a holistic and analytic assessment of and a grade on their third version. I both introduce revising strategies (including editing) to my students and also make suggestions for particular revisions, on things like word choice, articles, and prepositions, which are not so easily addressed by general strategies.

On the relationship between reader and writer: I talk to students explicitly about audience and purpose for their writing. I am inclined to ask students to write for their immediate peers (classmates) because I have become skeptical about the usefulness of having them write for a fictional audience, whether invoked by me or them. In general, I choose the real and present over the fictional and absent. And I am not all that bothered if students write for me for the purpose of getting a good grade—this strikes me as a perfectly reasonable move on their part, and after all, I think that I (along with most experienced writing teachers) am a good and resourceful reader who will be able to provide them with useful feedback. Then there's Aristotle (again): I find that the explicit introduction of the notion of appeals—ethos (to credibility), pathos (to emotion), and logos (to logic)—opens a lot of students' eyes and substantially enhances their rhetorical skills.

On texts: I look at student texts in terms of formal, functional, and generic features. Formal features include linguistic elements and conventions at or below the sentence level—for example, subject/verb agreement and comma usage. Functional features comprise inter- and extra-sentential elements, such as cohesion and coherence, introductions, and conclusions. Generic features involve characteristics of particular text types—for example, conventions of business letters and research proposals.

I examine textual features with the realization that there is a great deal of overlap among them. I do my best to provide students with advice and options, rather than dictates, on their work in progress. I believe that students should have the prerogative to ignore my suggestions and take responsibility for the texts they produce. In short, I try to model the situation wherein one asks a colleague to read and respond to a paper in progress. I also ask students to be proactive, that is, to let me know what textual elements they feel they are having difficulty with so that I can focus specifically on these when reading and responding to their papers. I am comfortable discussing common textual problems with my class as a whole or addressing individual issues one-on-one.

On contexts for teaching writing: I find it essential in planning and teaching writing courses to seriously consider context—institutional, societal, political, and ideological—and material conditions. For example, I need to consider how my teaching will be affected by the fact that I happen to work at a large, first-tier, science- and technology-oriented research university in a small town in the middle of the USA. I need to know something about how my students are regarded by and regard the societies of Purdue University; West Lafayette, Indiana; the Midwest; and the USA.

I try to remain cognizant of my own political and ideological proclivities and agendas—how they might be similar to or different from those of my students and how all of this affects my pedagogy. As for material conditions, it's important for me to understand the extent and limits of support that I get from the university as reflected by the space in which I'm expected to work, how many classes I'm expected to teach, the number of students in my classes, my access to technology, and other issues.

Finally, while I would not be so presumptuous as to try and tell other ESL writing teachers what to do, there are a few things I wish someone had told me when I started out—though I'm not sure I would have taken the advice offered. Anyway, here is what I wish I'd known.

- The prime directive: first, do no harm; do your best to make sure that students come out of your class feeling better about writing in English than when they came in.
- If you haven't done so already, do some writing in a second language: humbling experiences can be valuable.
- Treat your students like the sentient and complex individuals they are.
- Ask your students to tell you (better, write to you) about their previous experience with writing and their expectations about writing instruction.
- Listen to and think about what your students tell you about these things.
- Pay attention to and reflect on what happens in your classroom.
- Stay abreast of developments in the professional literature on writing (L1 and L2).

- Stay open to new ideas.
- Take from the literature only what you see as useful for you and your students in your instructional context.
- Avoid adopting a pedagogy just because it's enjoying its 15 minutes of fame.
- Integrate what you learn in the classroom with what you learn from the literature.
- Share what you have learned about writing with your students.
- Know that there are lots of different ways to help students improve their writing.
- Know that what you do—facilitating communication across languages and cultures—is noble and important work.
- Feel free to ignore all unsolicited advice.

References

Leki, I. (1991/92). Building authorial expertise through sequenced writing assignments. *TESOL Journal, 1(1)*, 19–23.

As the oldest of six children, Joy Reid has always been a teacher. Her professional experiences include teaching English at the largest high school in Missouri, then at possibly the smallest in Minnesota. Her ESL career began when a tornado destroyed the university where she had been hired part-time to teach composition. She is currently on leave from the University of Wyoming, working and reflecting in Hawaii, and teaching part-time at Maui Community College. Her intention is to finally finish her years'-long albatross project, an introductory book entitled Damnlinguistics.

Ask!

Joy Reid
University of Wyoming

Newly married in the 1960s, my husband and I would often find ourselves discussing our first-year composition classes over a quick casserole supper (with candles). I'd say, "If I could only teach my students to outline well, I know I could make them better writers." Steve would reply, "Outlining . . . so, ummm, structured . . . kinda suppresses creativity . . . but if I could teach my students to get all their ideas out, scribbled down without caring about structure, then select the best of their brainstorming for their papers. . . ." To which I might reply, "Brainstorming . . . so, ummm, messy."

Beginnings

In the 1960s, there were few experienced ESL composition specialists to be found, nor were any being educated at the time. In general, ESL instructors were prepared to teach grammar, reading, and oral skills, so their writing classes were planned around the language skills they were prepared to teach. In contrast, teachers of native English speaker (NES) composition employed in ESL writing classes were generally unaware of cultural differences, contrastive analysis, and contrastive rhetoric: their classes focused on writing skills needed by NESs but did not address the specialized needs of ESL students.

I belonged to the latter group when, in 1966, a tornado began my ESL career. That tornado killed 26 and partially destroyed Washburn University in Topeka (Kansas), where I had been hired to teach first-year composition, as my husband returned to graduate school. Distraught, I considered taking in laundry, then served as a grader at the University of Kansas (KU) and heard that the Applied English Center at KU needed teachers and that "You can earn while you learn." Armed only with my master's degree in English, two years of high-school teaching, and my background as an "Army brat," I took the ESL methods course and simultaneously began teaching the famed "Michigan method" (also discussed by Linda Lonon Blanton in her tale): my assignment was intermediate pattern practice and advanced writing.

I soon, however, discovered that the ESL "writing" class was not writing at all but rather a written grammar class, in which students practiced grammatical structures at the sentence level. Thus, I obediently asked ESL writing students to compose paragraphs in, for example, the past tense—until I tried to write such a paragraph myself. Then I complained to the director during a staff meeting that the approach was definitely not preparing students for first-year composition; I was assured that the Michigan method "worked." A year later, the KU English department grew frustrated with the large number of "problem" foreign students in first-year composition, so it registered those students for two separate sections and asked me to teach them.

In the late 1960s, composition at KU was literature based. Students read short stories, poetry, and a novel, and they followed their reading by writing literary analyses. My sections of composition were composed of 50 traditionally aged ESL students. About a third were from Venezuela; the rest came from countries in Asia and the Middle East. Early in the semester, I taught Hawthorne's "Young Goodman Brown" and found the class utterly confused. In answer to my questions, they said they had read and understood the words, but the meaning, well, . . . ? So for the next class, I prepared a 10-minute lecture on Puritanism to provide the necessary background. About 90 seconds into the lecture, students began glancing at each other; by the halfway mark, they were clearly incredulous, even rolling their eyes. Finally, the Venezuelan students began to laugh aloud and asked if what I had told them was "really true." Did Americans really "believe it"? I asked why my lecture seemed so funny, and the discussion that followed taught me more than it did the students, the first of many lessons in intercultural differences.

By the time my husband was offered a position at Colorado State University (CSU), I had developed a writing curriculum for the international-student sheltered-composition sections at KU. My resources included reading in NES composition theory and practice, evaluating hundreds of ESL and NES papers, and asking the ESL students questions—about the grammars of their first languages, about their responses to class content, and about their understanding of English structures: "Why did you capitalize all these words?" "Is this structure correct in your language?" "How do you do [X] in your first language?"

I worked hard to plan classes and organize teacher-centered structured classroom experiences that were also comfortable for students. I lectured, *questioned,* tested, graded, led discussions, conferenced, and answered questions. I learned not to be embarrassed by saying, "I don't know," especially when I realized I could learn the answer before the next class meeting. And I analyzed everything: whether or not the materials I developed worked and how to teach those materials better; why this student didn't learn; why an error kept occurring in that student's work; and how to teach still another student about Y or Z. I felt utterly responsible for "my" students' learning.

In retrospect, I had only just begun to realize how much the students knew. I *asked* the most basic of questions because I was ignorant and needed to know. But the students' answers gave me better ideas of what they didn't know and/or needed to know about academic writing. (And I hope that I made up for inexperience with enthusiasm and industry.)

Focus on ESL Student Writing

I realized early on that, despite my "standard" American English upbringing, my family used lay *and* lie *incorrectly. So I mostly avoided those words (and still do). But I was in my thirties before another English teacher pointed out that I was incorrectly using coordinate conjunctions after a semicolon and in my forties before my editor at Prentice-Hall informed me that only nonrestrictive relative clauses begin with "which."*

Although CSU offered a master's degree in TESL/TEFL, the university didn't have an intensive English program (IEP), so for a couple of years I returned to part-time teaching: NES composition and literature to nontraditionally aged students in the evening extension program. One of the mature students in a Women in Literature course proposed that she and I should write a romantic novel together. After confessing that I'd never read one, I read a dozen and decided that I could follow that recipe with ease. I was wrong. My coauthor pointed out that, in case I hadn't noticed (and I hadn't), paperback romances had (*a*) no semicolons and (*b*) an abnormal number of descriptive adjectives—my first lesson in discourse analysis. With that insight, I also realized that ESL teachers cannot expect their students to develop intuitions about grammar structures. Students need explicit information about grammar resources within the context of each assignment.

I also volunteered to teach the wives of international students at a local church. The students ranged from highly educated women who needed to escape married-student housing to many surprisingly young women who were illiterate in their first languages. My first assignment was a classic teacher's error: I assigned these homemakers to bring in their favorite recipe to share. Later in the semester, when the women felt more comfortable with me, I *asked* about their feelings about the class. Many explained that they had to enlist help from their husbands because (*a*) they didn't cook from written recipes (they'd learned from working alongside their mothers), (*b*) they didn't know English measuring units, (*c*) they didn't know the English names for many of the ingredients, (*d*) they had never encountered the convention for writing recipes, and (*e*) they couldn't write in English. My assignment had caused much family friction. In fact, several of the husbands had nearly decided that their wives could not return for more English lessons.

These experiences opened my eyes to the difficulties ESL students must have when they write academic prose. If an NES English teacher didn't notice her own incorrect punctuation and usage, if an NES English teacher simply avoided the two verbs she had learned incorrectly, if an NES English teacher could read a dozen romance novels and not notice the level of adjective use, then what about the ESL student who makes two-dozen errors in a single paper and doesn't have a clue how to correct them; or the ESL student who avoids using relative clauses because they don't occur in her language and she's not certain how they work; or the ESL student who, when *asked* why she capitalized in a way that seemed completely random, answered that the rule was to capitalize *i* (including each *i* at the beginning and in the middle of words)?

In my ongoing self-education, I also encountered the concept of contrastive rhetoric and knew intuitively that it was important. I began a career-long *questioning* of my students about organizational structures, "recipes" for formal writing in their first languages, and expectations of their native-speaker readers. I read and reread Mina Shaughnessy's *Errors and Expectations* (1977), a treasure trove before its time, and one that had a profound impact on Barbara Kroll as well, as she recounts. Shaughnessy characterizes student error this way: "Most students, whether they started out speaking Chinese or BEV [Black English Vernacular] or Navajo, seem to end up in freshman English with a common stock of errors that appear most often to arise directly from interference from other languages and dialects, from problems of predictability within the system called formal English, or from the difficulties associated with writing English rather than speaking it" (p. 157). Although Shaughnessy recognized that, for students, learning to correct errors is the least-rewarding part of writing (and hard work for little gain), she was convinced that the work was worth doing. I agreed with her then and still do.

Focus on Developing a Writing Curriculum and Materials

> In Vivian Zamel's case study of ESL student writers, published in the TESOL Quarterly (1983), her "least skilled writer admitted that she felt troubled by her inability to construct a plan on which to base her paper" (76). Zamel hypothesized that this student was hampered by previous writing teachers who constrained her creativity by forcing her to plan. However, I took the student at her word (that is, I "listened" to her): Developmentally, she had not yet achieved a level of writing skills and strategies that would allow her to feel confident about composing. She had only limited background information and no rhetorical framework within which to write.

In 1977, three part-time teachers and an English TESL/ TEFL faculty member founded the Colorado State University Intensive English Program (CSU/IEP). For the first semester, we recruited, planned curriculum, ordered books, and taught. The program grew. I became the writing-curriculum supervisor and the academic administrator, as well as a teacher. We drew interns and teaching assistants from the growing master's TESL/TEFL program. We located space and spent our meager funds making it viable, only to lose it to others who had more influence. We spent time in different units of the university, finally finding a permanent home in the English Department, with classrooms in the basement of the (eventually condemned) statistics building. In 1980, I attended my first International TESOL Convention. I tried to attend a relevant session on writing during every presentation period and arrived home exhausted but filled with exciting information to share with our IEP writing faculty.

In the late 1970s, very few ESL writing textbooks existed. The one I finally found for the advanced ESL writing course was *American English Rhetoric* by Robert Bander (1971), a book I ultimately found irrelevant to the tasks assigned in first-year composition. (Ann Johns and Barbara Kroll also write about Bander in this collection.) As I gained experience in the classroom, I began to develop my own materials at what turned out to be an alarming rate. Eventually a small group of students told me that their dormitory rooms were becoming a "fire hazard" because of all my handouts. (The following summer I pulled those materials together and sent the entire manuscript directly to a publisher, not realizing that the "over the transom" submission was culturally inappropriate. The manuscript later became *The Process of Composition,* an advanced ESL writing textbook now in its third edition [Reid, 2000]).

My materials development was based on my NES composition teaching experience, as well as my IEP experience, and I *asked* the ESL students to bring writing assignments from other university classes they were taking so that we could study those assignments together. Our discussions fueled my interest in what students actually had to write in their university courses. The result for me was a commitment to pragmatism. That is, I couldn't teach everything about writing; I couldn't mark every error in every paper. But by analyzing the tasks their university classes required, I could focus on identifying and analyzing the writing skills needed to complete those tasks.

Continuing to Learn

I continued to *ask* students to evaluate the worth and clarity of my materials: Was this assignment clear? Interesting? Did this explanation of clauses "work"? Why or why not? What about this exercise—was it helpful or not? I began to work with error analysis in and out of class, and I *asked* whether or not students understood the errors I marked on their papers: Why do you think this is an error? Do you know how to correct the error? I was often as amazed at my students' insights and explanations as I was horrified by the rules they sometimes gave me about their errors: "You always have to put a comma after *and*" or "You have to put a comma after descriptive words like *beautiful.*"

In addition to conducting my own studies in error analysis, I continued reading in the fields of NES composition and ESL composition, each of which by then had started to accumulate its own body of literature. Some of the literature suggested that, for several reasons, not only might I want to refrain from marking every error in every paper (and still have a life) but I should *not* mark every error. As most researchers and ESL teachers agreed, marking errors that students could neither recognize nor correct was an exercise in futility and frustration. Some teachers reported that many students could not tolerate the explosion of marks: facing all those revisions was more than they could handle. Further, research had begun to demonstrate that ESL error, written or spoken, was not deviant but rather one of several processes through which students developed their language skills. In fact, errors represented stages in language growth, a kind of "interlanguage." The errors might actually be the product of intelligent choices by a writer, instead of a failure to understand rules, a point suggested by Shaughnessy (1977).

Finally, several small investigations (see, e.g., Vann, Meyer, & Lorenz, 1984) indicated that errors were hierarchical. That is, some were more "irritating" to academic readers than others, and some were more crucial to comprehension than others. In terms of irritation, the studies suggested that errors not associated with NES writing were more bothersome, regardless of their comprehensibility (or lack thereof). Included were errors in article and preposition use, as well as inappropriate word forms. Generally speaking, the studies showed that the use of incorrect vocabulary (the wrong word) seemed most likely to interfere with communication; verb-tense errors also often contributed to reader confusion.

In *asking* students about the concept of error gravity, I discovered that none had ever even considered the possibility that errors should or could be prioritized. Further, we discussed the cost-benefit ratio of errors: that the time put into remediation should not exceed the importance (or unimportance) of that error. For example, for students whose first languages do not include articles and/or prepositions, such errors can take a lifetime and more to remediate. Better, perhaps, to spend time on errors that are both important and correctable within a shorter period of time.[1] Generally, students were relieved that they could select more crucial grammar problems to remediate. They could make a revision plan rather than experiencing the overwhelming feeling of "all those mistakes!"

In several classes I *asked* students to help with the revisions of my ESL writing textbooks by (*a*) evaluating the interest and usefulness of exercises and assignments, (*b*) identifying difficult concepts that needed additional practice, and (*c*) writing and/or selecting new student samples for the revisions. I found their information both trustworthy and perceptive, and their writing improved as they competed for "publication." Students seemed delighted with the opportunities to become part of the teaching process; for them, the authenticity of their work was highly motivating.

In addition, by *asking* students about their assumptions about writing instruction, I discovered that many entered writing classes with incorrect, usually unarticulated, and sometimes astounding assumptions that could profoundly affect their success in the class. Among them:

- Every writing task is a brand-new ball game, so why spend time learning skills and strategies that won't transfer to other academic assignments?
- There are no real grading standards; all teachers grade subjectively, and that's why a paper that received a C in one class may receive an A in another.
- When writing teachers write, they have virtually no problems composing, organizing, and revising. Their first draft is perfect.
- If the teacher shares some imperfect drafts of her writing, she is not to be trusted to teach writing.
- Teachers know all the secrets of writing effective academic prose *but will not tell the students.* Instead, students have to keep guessing at "what she wants," which they can try to do by analyzing the teacher's responses to their writing and the grades their papers receive.

I remember, too, during those teaching years, that I began to *inquire* about student knowledge concerning the audiences and purposes for U.S. academic writing (see Reid, 1989). Not surprisingly, I found that almost all ESL students lacked NES intuition about U.S. academic audiences and conventions. Because so few of the students had studied writing in their first languages, most had never considered either audience or purpose in any language. They were not, however, reluctant to learn. In fact, they were eager, or at the very least willing. That discovery led to an epiphany: I realized that no student deliberately wrote a poor paper; no student came to class not to learn; no student tried to make no progress. Instead, students' intentions were positive, and in answering my *questions,* they made their needs clear: they needed transparent information and explicit description of appropriate choices, and they liked models of academic writing by ESL and NES students, not in their class, who had acquired the skills they were practicing. After that, during almost every semester, students in my writing classes asked, "Why didn't someone tell us about this before? It's not really that hard after all."

Focus on Students as Learners

> *I am a field-independent, analytic, visual, Type-A, ENTJ (extroverted, intuitive, thinking, judging) learner. As a language learner, I prefer sequenced, deductive presentations of individual materials with carefully controlled practice. Approaches that include immersion, impulsivity, holistic and inductive presentation of materials, learning through listening exclusively, and high-risk practice frighten and repel me.*

An offhand conversation with my sister led me into research on learning styles, an area that has become one of my main scholarly concerns. As a vocational educator, my sister had received, as a conference handout, a learning-styles survey designed for NES public schools. Intrigued, I shared it with my intermediate and advanced ESL writing students. They completed the survey, responded to its results in writing, and then evaluated their experiences with their own survey. The initial surprise of the students about the existence of learning styles paralleled my own. I *asked* them to experiment with me—to become partners in learning—to discover more about learning academic writing by identifying and implementing their stronger and weaker styles, then evaluating their experiences.

I studied their interpretations and evaluations, developing materials and teaching methods that appealed to a variety of learning styles, seeking to integrate my teaching of writing skills and strategies with students' styles. Students' positive reactions and discussions also led me to develop and norm a learning-styles survey for ESL students: the Perceptual Learning Styles Preference Survey (PLSPS; see Reid, 1987). Another consequence: a shift from my interest in *teaching* ESL writing to a focus on how individual students *learn*. I began reading and writing about student needs, learning and teaching styles, and learning and teaching strategies (see Reid, 1995, 1998b).

These experiences, as well as the TESL/TEFL literature, led me to a definition of the "student-centered" classroom: one in which students, as well as teachers, have responsibilities that function almost as a mutually agreed-upon contract. In simple terms, the teacher must be well versed in the material, willing and able to teach, and trained in methods and approaches that can help students construct opportunities for learning. Students are expected to be well prepared, be willing to learn and experiment and evaluate, and be ready to take advantage of learning opportunities. In other words, students are responsible for their own learning or for the consequences of not learning. The correlate is the formation, development, and maintenance of a classroom community, by both teachers and students, in which each student has strengths and weaknesses, so each has contributions to make—in class discussions and in pair and group work—as well as concepts, skills, and information to learn.

The Processes of Change

> *My son Michael, then 20, and two college friends stand awk-wardly in the living room, responding to introductions to some ESL writing teachers, who are meeting there to discuss curriculum. As they leave, Michael says to his friends, "Do you remember when we had to do all that c——— in freshman English, like brainstorming and outlining?" And they laugh, knowingly.*

My interests in student learning helped me make the decision to return to school part-time to earn a doctorate, to see firsthand from the "other side of the desk" how learning styles affect student success. In one of my classes, I also began learning about the change process. As with my encounters with contrastive rhetoric and learning styles, I realized the importance of change in the classroom and particularly in students' learning processes. After all, education *is* change. Further, some of the tenets of change, among them the following, seem especially relevant to the ESL writing class:

- *Change isn't easy.* While some may initially report that they "love" change, that change is life and so should be expected and appreciated, the fact is that even small changes take time, patience, and resources.[2] How much greater are the multiple changes that ESL students face as they strive to adjust the presentation of their ideas to the conventions of another language and culture!
- *Change isn't a single event.* Rather, it more closely resembles a nonlinear process: two steps forward, one step back. Research shows that any change—beginning a diet or a marriage, using a new textbook or curriculum, starting college or a job—involves several recursive stages. The first of these is

an information stage, followed by the most crucial, a personal stage, in which students commit to the change (the learning).

- *Real change occurs only if the person changing can see and accept the benefits of that change.* Teachers too can benefit from understanding the change process; and by describing these processes to students, they can empower their students. As a result, when student attitudes turn sour, teachers and students can recognize the symptoms, and teachers will not take the symptoms personally. Rather, they can offer appropriate encouragement and support.

According to student answers to my many *questions,* ESL writers initially have high expectations for success. However, as the workload increases and the mastery of writing skills and strategies becomes more complex, even students who remain committed to learning may not see improvement in their writing. Indeed, as they risk more change, they may make more errors, so their writing may seem "worse." In reaction, students may escape backwards—into previous writing skills and strategies. Feelings of fear and failure may assail some students; others may blame the teacher, the textbook, and/or the English language for their frustrations. Further, students who may not understand that these change processes are normal may even feel guilty about feeling negative and resentful.

In contrast to real change, imposed change is not very successful, although it can appear to work, at least at first. Without "buy-in," a student may *behave*—that is, perform the change on cue—but she or he will not *become.* Similar to what my son and his friends expressed (see the beginning of this section), the change will not be permanent. But if students are aware of the stages of change, and they know these stages are normal and transient, they can share their feelings, write about them, and see the end of the proverbial tunnel.

If it sounds as though I hammered my ESL writing classes

with hours of work on learning styles and strategies, then lectured them interminably about the change process, to the exclusion of teaching writing, let me dispel that myth. I used learning styles as content for a single set of writing assignments, and I confined discussion of the change process to three short discussions (10–15 minutes each) during the semester. However, both have become integral to my teaching philosophy, as important as contrastive rhetoric, as NES composition practices, as research in curriculum design, and as my own lesson planning.

Writing and the Academic World

I'd been invited to do a lunchtime "brown-bag" presentation at the Center for Applied Linguistics (CAL). My presentation related to a finding of my dissertation research on discourse analysis, namely that native speakers of Arabic, when writing in English, tend to use coordinate structures in longer strings than U.S. academic readers find acceptable (clause, and clause, and clause, so clause, but clause, and clause). I suggested that ESL writing teachers should demonstrate for their Arabic-speaking students ways to subordinate clauses so that their sentences did not sound so "childish" to U.S. academic readers. A native Arabic speaker working at CAL replied, "Now I understand why the native English speakers learning to write in Arabic use so many relative clauses that sound so, ummm, 'childish' in Arabic."

A decade ago, I turned my research and reading to the academic world outside the ESL writing classroom. I investigated major curricular challenges such as the development of the most efficient, effective methods to sequence and spiral academic writing tasks (see Reid, 2001); the processes to determine how to prepare students to successfully enter the academic discourse community; and the differences between international students, whom I classified as "eye learners," and U.S. resident students, whom I categorized (along a continuum) as "ear learners" (Reid, 1998a). In the classroom, I discussed writing issues with students that continued to present problems: the use of specific detail (how much? what kind?); appropriate citation use (what kind? when? how?); analysis of student meta-cognition to develop critical thinking and student responsibility; and successful revision skills.

Further, my developing philosophy of pragmatism led me to investigate some of the macro-questions that still exist in teaching (and learning) ESL writing; questions like these:

1) *What effective writing skills demonstrate mature U.S. academic writing?* That is, what syntactic and rhetorical information should ESL writers learn and practice in order to produce the writing expected by NES academic readers? As demonstrated in the example of Arabic and English (at the beginning of this section), grammatical patterns and structures may well be valued differently across cultures.

Early NES research indicated that longer sentences, with more subordination, increase the perceived sophistication of academic writing (Mellon, 1969; O'Hare, 1974). More recent investigation has been concerned with the numerous differences, even in syntax, in writing across the disciplines. For example, laboratory reports in the sciences conventionally contain passive voice and not the first-person singular ("I"), yet passive voice is often denigrated by writing teachers. Research has shown that relative clauses often expand description in academic writing considered "mature," that appositives are among the most frequently used structures to identify the credibility of authoritative sources, and that prepositional phrases frequently act as transitions. And some geology journals even "permit" authors to use exclamation points!

Borrowing a word from literature, these conventions (and the syntactic structures that accompany them) are termed *genres*. Discipline-specific conventions that are characteristic (in content, organization, and form) of various genres emerge from social practice, as discussed by Ann M. Johns in this collection. By *asking* (of course), I found that the students were as unfamiliar with these various conventions of academic genres as I was. The challenge, then, for ESL students and teachers is clear: How to identify academic genre conventions, and how to practice and produce them successfully? NES and ESL research has expanded my own knowledge of disciplinary genres, and I recommend to new teachers of ESL that they investigate this research too (especially Biber, Conrad, & Reppen, 1998; Hyland, 2001; Hyon, 1996; Swales, 1990).

2) *What writing tasks will ESL students actually encounter in their university courses?* My ESL writing classes have never existed in a vacuum; my objective has always been to prepare students for academic writing. The hundreds of academic writing assignments I have *asked* students to bring me over 30 years form a basis for my knowledge in this area. In addition, published research about NES and ESL writing assignments has increased, and a large-scale investigation sponsored by the Educational Testing Service (Hale *et al.*, 1996) lends additional information to my informal database.

From others' research and my own investigation, I have learned the following about the way academic writing functions in academe: (*a*) A major function of writing assignments is to provide students an opportunity to demonstrate knowledge and/or skills; in other words, academic writing is a form of testing. (*b*) Most topics for writing in academic classes are assigned; few allow choice, and then only within a limited scope. (*c*) In-class writing assignments are almost solely short-answer tasks and essays. And (*d*) the most common out-of-class assignments include these: summaries, with or without analysis (including book reviews/critiques); reports, with interpretation; plans/proposals; and library research papers. If these results prove consistent in future research—and my students think they will—curriculum, textbooks, and theories of teaching ESL writing need to be reexamined. It seems logical to form a skills-and-strategies taxonomy that can be sequenced and spiraled through an ESL writing curriculum.

3) *What writing skills are transferable from one academic writing task to another?* Given the results of research about writing assignments, this question follows logically. Are there subskills and discourse literacies that students can use in a variety of writing situations? Do subtechnical vocabulary and grammar clusters cross disciplines (Byrd, 1998)? Research is limited but suggests that, for example, the overall organization of *introduction, background, body paragraphs,* and *conclusion* probably fits most academic papers, from the five-paragraph essay, to a social science research paper, to a research report, to a master's thesis. Functions of organizational sections are probably similar. An introduction, for instance, functions to (*a*) introduce the general topic, (*b*) engage the reader by giving a little information about the specific topic, and (*c*) announce the overall thesis of the paper to follow. Library and Internet research strategies—including citation skills, identification and analysis of audience expectations, analysis of sample authentic assignments, the construction and use of nontext materials (graphs, illustrations, timelines, etc.), transition relationships, persuasive techniques, summary skills, and analysis/synthesis techniques—all appear to be subskills that can be transferred to and used in a variety of writing assignments.

Conclusion

Two final reflections: (*a*) the longer I teach, the less I appear to teach, but the more I provide opportunities for learning; and (*b*) teaching ESL writing is never boring. And what of the future? My hope is that research will allow teachers to determine more specifically the roles of rhetorical, contextual, and linguistic tasks and skills across disciplinary genres.

I look forward to longitudinal studies of ESL student writers similar to Marilyn Sternglass's (1997) work with NES writers and to additional work discovering what writing skills and subskills are most important for academic writing. Future research in error analysis and error gravity, as well as ongoing research in responding to student writing, could help both teacher and student. And I will continue to *ask,* because I believe that students are our best resources. They have many of our answers.[3]

Notes

1. My suggestion to students about articles and prepositions was (and continues to be) to locate NESs and ask them, as a favor, to proofread for just those errors. The NESs must not use a writing instrument; only the ESL writer can make the changes. I call it "pizza for proofing" and insist that the ESL student be present during the process, offering perhaps to buy the NES helper a pizza in exchange for the work.

2. To demonstrate, try a small, chosen change in your life and then reflect on the energy needed and your feelings as you choose to implement the change. For instance, for the rest of your day, try folding your arms across your chest the opposite way from your habitual folding; or, on your way home tonight, take a slightly different route; or, tomorrow morning, try brushing your teeth a different way.

3. I am not usually a "discovery" writer. However, as I reread this essay, I made several discoveries. First, any writing about one's personal or professional life appears to be chronological but is really an overlapping, recursive effort with an artificial timeline imposed on it. My story in this collection is no exception. But despite the arbitrary linear flow, I was surprised to find that my professional development has expanded from a focus on classroom content to include students' needs and then further to encompass the expectations and values of the institutions that exist around and outside an ESL program. I also discovered the emergence of two themes. One, I discovered that asking has been an important part of my pedagogy, especially my questioning of students and discussions with them. And two, perhaps because I continue to teach writing every year, I see that I am, ultimately, a classroom researcher, interested primarily in improving course materials and students' learning. I did not see all of this in such clear relief before setting out to compose this essay.

References

Bander, R. G. (1971). *American English rhetoric.* New York: Holt, Rinehart, Winston.

Biber, D., Conrad, S., & Reppen, R. (1998). *Corpus linguistics: Investigating language structure and use.* Cambridge, UK: Cambridge University Press.

Byrd, P. (1998). Grammar in the composition syllabus. In P. Byrd & J. Reid, (Eds.), *Grammar in the composition classroom* (pp. 33–53). Boston: Heinle & Heinle.

Hale, G., Taylor, C., Bridgeman, B., Carson, J., Kroll, B., & Kantor, R. (1996). *A study of writing tasks assigned in academic degree programs.* TOEFL Research Report 54. Princeton, NJ: Educational Testing Service.

Hyland, K. (2001). Disciplinary discourses: Writer stance in research articles. In C. Candlin & K. Hyland (Eds.), *Writing: Texts, processes, and practices* (pp. 99–121). London: Longman.

Hyon, S. (1996). Genre in three traditions: Implications for ESL. *TESOL Quarterly, 30,* 693–722.

Mellon, J. (1969). *Transformational sentence combining.* Urbana, IL: National Council of Teachers of English.

O'Hare, F. (1974). *Sentence combining: Improving student writing without formal grammar instruction.* Urbana, IL: National Council of Teachers of English.

Reid, J. (1987). The learning style preferences of ESL students. *TESOL Quarterly, 21,* 87–111.

Reid, J. (1989). English as a second language composition in higher education: The expectations of the academic audience. In D. M. Johnson & D. H. Roen (Eds.), *Richness in writing: Empowering ESL students* (pp. 220–234). New York: Longman.

Reid, J. (Ed.) (1995). *Learning styles in the ESL/EFL classroom.* Boston: Heinle & Heinle.

Reid, J. (1998a). "Eye" learners and "ear" learners: Identifying the language needs of international student and U.S. resident writers. In P. Byrd & J. Reid (Eds.), *Grammar in the composition classroom* (pp. 3–17). New York: Heinle & Heinle.

Reid, J. (Ed.). (1998b). *Understanding learning styles in the second language classroom.* Upper Saddle River, NJ: Prentice-Hall Regents.

Reid, J. (2000). *The process of composition* (3rd ed.). White Plains, NY: Prentice-Hall Regents.

Reid, J. (2001). Advanced EAP writing and curriculum design: What do we need to know? In T. Silva & P. K. Matsuda (Eds.), *On second language writing* (pp. 143–160). Mahwah, NJ: Lawrence Erlbaum Associates.

Shaughnessy, M. (1977). *Errors and expectations: A guide for the teacher of basic writing.* New York: Oxford University Press.

Sternglass, M. (1997). *Time to know them: A longitudinal study of writing and learning at the college level.* Mahwah, NJ: Lawrence Erlbaum Associates.

Swales, J. (1990). *Genre analysis: English in academic and research settings.* Cambridge: Cambridge University Press.

Vann, R. J., Meyer, D. E., & Lorenz, F. O. (1984). Error gravity: A study of faculty opinion of ESL errors. *TESOL Quarterly, 18,* 427–440.

Zamel, V. (1983). The composing processes of advanced ESL students: Six case studies. *TESOL Quarterly, 17,* 165–187.

When Ann M. Johns was considering a profession, she was told by her high school counselor that women should be nurses, teachers, or, perhaps, social workers, "so you can have something to fall back on if your husband dies." So she chose teaching. After four years as a teacher of eighth grade, she decided that if only her students were a bit older. . . . And that's how it all began.

A Story of Experimentation and Evolving Awareness,
Or Why I Became an Advocate for Approaching Writing through Genre

Ann M. Johns
San Diego State University

Like most of my colleagues who began to teach ESL/EFL composition in the dim, dark past—or even more recently— my story does not include ever having taken a reading or writing course, much less a course on teaching these "skills" to ESL/EFL students. Most of us are self-taught, products of departments of linguistics, foreign languages, education, or TESL/TEFL, where the emphases have been, and in some cases still are, on sentence-level grammar, literature, or methodologies for teaching second language speaking and listening. Only relatively recently have some graduate programs in TESOL begun to offer courses designed to deal specifically with the teaching of writing. But many other departments still continue to ignore issues of written literacy for second language students, providing no coursework or experiences to help prepare future L2 writing teachers.

An example from my own experience may illustrate the last point. Because I have directed my campus writing across the curriculum (WAC) program, I was asked by a colleague to contribute a chapter on ESL in the university classroom to a volume called *WAC for the New Millennium* (Johns, 2001a). In preparation for this chapter, I went on the electronic WAC listserv and asked faculty teaching first language composition to tell me about their experiences with ESL students. I got the usual responses: students plagiarize, faculty don't know how to deal with second language errors, and "students can't read!" One response was particularly strident: "I direct a writing program, and I *never* permit graduate students from the MA/TESOL program to teach in our classes. They have had no courses in the teaching of writing, and they insist on turning all their classes into grammar practice sessions!"

But back to my story, which, I hope you will notice, turns on the influence of context and the culture of writers upon text—a foreshadowing of my current emphasis upon genre studies and student inquiry. More than 40 years ago (gulp!), I married this guy, David, who likes to travel, so he designed a Ph.D. dissertation that required him to hit the road. It turned out that the roads I hit with him eventually took me for considerable periods of time to Africa and my first language-teaching experiences, to Chicago and San Diego, to the Middle East, and to China. In each of these locales, I taught literacy or taught teachers of literacy. Every experience fed into my growing understanding of the complexities of foreign/second language writing and reading and what it means to teach literacy or train others to undertake that teaching. In telling my story, I hope to show how my own thinking about the complexity and cultural situatedness of L2 reading and writing has matured to a point where I am convinced that our central task as teachers is to encourage students' flexibility and inquiry as they face a variety of literacy tasks and genres in their school and work.

Living, Teaching, and Learning in East Africa

David's dissertation topic, "Juu ya Siasa ya Afrika ya Mashariki" (On the Politics of East Africa—OK, he wrote it in English, not Swahili), enabled us to spend a year in Great Britain, where I studied Swahili at the University of London School of Oriental and African Studies. Another year was spent in East Africa, where I was a teacher at a British girls' school in colonial Kenya, the Lord Delamere. There, I taught history, my undergraduate major, because, as my British colleagues remarked, I didn't speak English, "only American." It was a bit stifling teaching colonial girls, so I helped out a missionary friend by teaching in a school for African children of prostitutes near a British air base. At that school, I taught (very) basic story-based literacies to the Kikuyu-speaking boys and girls, who were eager to learn and break from the profession of their mothers.

Later, when we moved to Uganda, I used the same, self-taught technique that had worked with the Kenyan children to teach adult students, many of whom were delighted to tell their stories for literacy practice. I learned later that the technique I had somehow intuitively developed for these classes closely resembles the Language Experience Approach (LEA) (see, e.g., Dixon & Nessel, 1983). In both Kenya and Uganda, I asked groups of students in the class to tell a story, either a fable or one of their own experiences. I then recorded the story, corrected and typed it up at home, made copies, bought pencils and paper, and assisted the students in copying the texts I had duplicated. They drew pictures to illustrate the texts and often accompanied them with a song while presenting them to the class. They also practiced writing selected vocabulary and reading the texts aloud.

When students finished the course, they had a "portfolio" of their story texts that they could read to their families.

It seemed to work, despite my lack of training or educational resources—perhaps because my students were so hungry to learn. To this day, I continue to recommend LEA to graduate students who are teaching new immigrants and refugees in the United States because it requires drawing from students' own texts and experiences, thus responding to their culture and interests.

Experimenting with Literary Genres

When David and I left East Africa, having witnessed Kenya's independence, we returned to the United States, where I continued my efforts to earn a Ph.T. ("Putting Him Through"—his doctorate) by teaching eighth-grade English (literature, of course) and history to a group of recalcitrant, English-speaking boys and girls in Chicago. As was the case in East Africa, I had no instruction in teaching literature or composition. I also had very little assistance from my more experienced colleagues, who seemed to favor grammar worksheets and story timelines in their language-arts classes.

In Africa, I had begun to realize the importance of the interaction between text content, organization, and the culture that the text embodied. In addition, I vaguely understood what has now become quite clear to me: students need to have genre experiences with different text formats, conventions, audiences, and writer purposes. They also need to talk about these differences, developing a metalanguage (that is, a way of talking about language) to discuss their genre analyses.

What was the first discipline to discuss texts and genres? Literature, of course. So I used genre models from the literature textbooks (fables, short stories, haiku, etc.), asking students to analyze these texts and model their own writing (in terms of structure and other conventions) after the textbook examples. I evaluated my eighth-graders' papers analytically (where did I learn that?), with different scores for text structure, content, reader interest, and editing. This grading system and the literature textbook I was using made me more secure than I had been in East Africa. At least at that point, the students and I had some models, so we knew what the required genres might look like and how language might be employed to achieve appropriate effects.

The principal and curriculum coordinators at my school seemed to like my approach, and none of the more involved parents complained. However, when I strayed from teaching literature, realizing, even then, that students need to use writing to get things done, I was chastised. I particularly remember a situation when the students in my class wrote to the congressman for their district about education issues that concerned them. The recipient, and the principal, informed me that these were not appropriate classroom activities. (To quote the congressman, "Your students are not old enough to vote or understand the issues. They should not be writing these letters.") Hmmm.

Some Real-World Experience with Genres in Context

David finished his dissertation (in 1965) and got a job at San Diego State University, where I was told to join the wives' group and play good bridge to enhance my husband's possibilities for promotion. I played lousy bridge, but I followed the other standard rules and produced a couple of children, devoting my time to attempting to mold their little lives, which, as all parents know, is a very humbling exercise.[1] Staying at home provided opportunities to volunteer, so I became active in the League of Women Voters (LWV), where I was introduced to genres central to politics and the law. I remember vividly one text, an *amicus curiae*—or friend of the court—brief entered on behalf of a local school-integration case.

There were also other LWV genres to write in: letters requesting contributions, memos to the officers, and position papers. Initially, these were unfamiliar genres, so I began to develop strategies for producing successful texts, that is, papers the appropriate audiences would read and be persuaded by. Like my current students, I studied successful texts from the genres I wanted to write in, and I tested my texts on experienced readers before sending them off.

Off to Egypt

While I raised children and worked with the LWV, the Vietnam War began to heat up. After the Democratic Convention of 1968, my husband and I decided we were sufficiently unhappy with the current political situation to leave the country, children and all. So we did: off to Egypt (1970–72), where David taught at the American University of Cairo (AUC), and the children attended a Lycée Française (where they learned Arabic, mostly).

My life and teaching perspectives began to change when I was invited to begin a master's program in TEFL at AUC. The master's students were required to teach writing to Arabic-speaking Egyptian students, but I was poorly prepared for the needs of the technically oriented students in my classes. How do you teach such a literate group? Not with the story-driven Language Experience Approach I had used in East Africa and certainly not with the genre studies in literature that had been my approach when teaching eighth-grade English speakers.

Our composition program director, who happened to be a nun from the University of Iowa, made the choice for us. She insisted on a "copy and compose" technique so that students would produce perfect, if dull and irrelevant, artificial texts. We graduate students rebelled, joining visiting professor Clifford Prator (UCLA) in developing a new writing program for freshmen. With Dr. Prator, who also figures prominently in

Melinda Erickson's story in this collection, we designed a test based on error analysis, spending hours classifying the errors from students' papers. Coincidentally, as recounted in her story, Barbara Kroll was teaching in an Israeli university during the exact same period, and her work was error oriented, as well.

I felt uncomfortable with this grammar-based emphasis however. Our students were in biology and engineering, but their needs had not been analyzed at all. Why weren't we working with their reading and writing texts? Why were our analyses so bottom-up, ignoring the importance of context, text structure, and content, not to mention the writer's purposes and audience? Rather surreptitiously, I began to collect their lab reports and other genres in English—as well as talk to them about the various texts they read and wrote in Arabic.

Building Profession and Place

By the mid-1970s, my husband and I had returned to San Diego. The children were in school, and I had a new MA in TEFL. As a result of my Egyptian experience, I did know more about teaching literacy, and I had learned a great deal from my Egyptian and Palestinian friends about reading and writing in a foreign language. So I began the "freeway bracero" work so common throughout the United States: teaching all types of ESL classes in adult school, in community college, and, on a volunteer basis, at San Diego State. San Diego is a great town for immigrants, so I was in considerable demand as an ESL teacher.

At that point, my pedagogical guide in all of the writing classes, whatever the level, was one of the most popular ESL writing volumes available at the time, one also remembered vividly by Barbara Kroll: Robert Bander's *American English Rhetoric* (1971), which garnered so much money for the author that he retired on it. And for its time, it *was* a good book: a structuralist text with many exercises and examples for writing in the "modes" (e.g., definition, example, cause and effect, comparison and contrast). Bander certainly did not stint on models for writing, on which I continued to rely. My students and I particularly liked "Lincoln and Grant at Appomattox" by Bruce Catton, used as an example of comparison/contrast.

I learned a great deal from this ESL text, about writing exercises, text structures (now called "strategies" in many current writing textbooks), and text analysis. I do not regret those years, though my ESL students, always tolerant, must have become tired of attempting to fit their thoughts into preconceived and often unnatural structures such as comparison/contrast and cause/effect. They also must have asked themselves, "So what does this really have to do with the academic and professional writing I will be doing in my life?" Had they asked out loud, I would not have been able to provide them with an adequate answer.

When I teach ESL/EFL reading and writing pedagogy to current graduate students, I use Bander as an example of that period. My experienced students tell me that his "current-traditional" approach is alive and well at every level of instruction (see Silva, 1990, for a discussion of these approaches). After all, what is the five-paragraph essay but a structural container into which students pour content? I always point out, however, that though text structure and the purposes it serves are central to students' understanding of genres, they are only part of the story. As we write, we must also consider audience, immediate context, content—and our own intent.

One of my dreams during this period was to become a real (that is, tenured) faculty member at San Diego State, where teaching and research are both highly valued and intellectual discussion, even of the teaching of writing, had become commonplace. So I took on a few more responsibilities, hoping to be noticed. In 1973, I founded the American

Language Institute for the university and delved into English for Specific Purposes (see Swales, 1988, for a history; Dudley-Evans & St. John, 1998, for principles and current trends).

ESP was a great financial boon for the institute, which immediately began developing special courses for business, engineering, and other disciplines attractive to international students. Functional expository writing was central to these ESP efforts, and it was much more interesting to me personally than oral language. ESP gave me no choice but to think seriously about students' needs, the contexts in which they would read and write, and the genres appropriate for these contexts. I began to publish, first about students and their attempts to write in genres, and then about more theoretical issues.

At that point in my life, still hoping to advance to regular faculty tenure-track status, I began a Ph.D. program at the University of Southern California, where I was lucky enough to have Robert Kaplan on my dissertation committee. I was one of many people throughout the world who benefited from Bob's gruff mentoring and constant support and will be forever in his debt. (He was also the person who indirectly brought Barbara Kroll into her studies of rhetoric and linguistics.)

While I was commuting to Los Angeles for classes, attempting to raise a family (now three children), and keep David moderately happy, I continued to teach at least one ESL writing class in what was then the Academic Skills Center at San Diego State. Since the English Department had dumped the "remedial" writing and ESL programs in the early 1970s because its faculty argued they had more important work to do at the university than "teach those students who don't belong here," the Academic Skills Center agreed, quite willingly, to take responsibility for remediation and ESL—and so there was plenty of ESL writing to be taught. The English Department's general reluctance to view writing as distinct from literature and their unwillingness to consider the teaching of remedial and ESL students eventually caught up with them in the early 1990s, however. A group of faculty, of which I was a part, proposed a Department of Rhetoric and Writing Studies, combining the work of the Academic Skills Center and the composition classes in the English Department to create a new administrative unit. The formation of this department and the angry and persistent opposition by English departments across the California State University system to this move is another story, too long and sordid to tell. (However, see Little & Rose, 1994, for an account by the two faculty from English who wrote the original department proposal.)

Perhaps the most interesting part, beyond the remarkable documents this effort produced, is the support the rest of the university faculty and administration afforded during the formative period. The engineering, business, sciences, and social sciences faculty believed that if the teaching of writing were separated from English, students would have more respect for and practice in writing and for the genres of the various disciplines and professions represented at the university. We hope their faith in our department has been justified.

Serial Flirtations with Methods and Textbooks

When I began to teach for the Academic Skills Center (1973), what was recommended for writing classes? By then, ESL textbooks had caught up with the 1960s, at their most extreme, with the expressivist approaches (see Silva, 1990; Johns, 1990, 1997). Textbooks and teacher guides encouraged students to "find their own voices." Writing was about self-expression and waiting for the muse to provide inspiration. In complete contrast to Bander's approach, which had relied on rhetorical models, we were asked *not* to provide models or assist students with organizing texts because this guidance would "stifle student voices." Text structure and grammar were to follow the meaning created by the writer (Zamel, 1982). Nothing, certainly not the teacher, was to get in the way of students' own interests and efforts to express themselves.

Still untenured, I tried to be "hip," assigning open journal writing and open topics for papers—even tempting the muse with pictures and films. However, I always felt like I was cheating students, not telling them about academic writing or helping them organize their writing to be effective for various audiences and contexts. Since they were ESL and bilingual students, they often couldn't find structures to follow meaning because they didn't know enough about the grammar or genres of English to be independent from guidance. Unfortunately, when the students were tested for proficiency by the university, they were expected to know, and use, common text structures and argumentation.[2]

Throughout this period, my students' insistent request, particularly in the face of the evaluation system, was "just tell me how to do it." I explained that by actually directing, rather than merely facilitating, their writing, I would be drying up their creative juices. Most of my students didn't buy that argument. So I came to the conclusion that though students' "voices" needed to be heard, if students were to succeed, both in the university and beyond, they needed to have more than a personal voice and more in the classroom than sufficient opportunities to evoke the muse.[3] What they needed, among other things, were experiences and opportunities for analysis with a variety of genres.

Still hoping that the experts would give me the answers, I moved on in the late 1970s and throughout the 1980s to the next possibility in textbooks, those promoting a "process approach," perhaps the greatest contribution to the teaching of writing in our short ESL composition history (see Silva, 1990; Johns, 1990). What was the "writing process," as portrayed in many ESL textbooks? It included some kind of prewriting activity (such as brainstorming), an initial student draft of the paper, peer review of the draft, revision, and final editing for sentence-level errors. There was a problem, however. Although research into actual student writing was beginning in earnest (see, e.g., Raimes, 1985; Spack, 1984; and Zamel, 1983), textbooks and classroom approaches at that time did not necessarily reflect the complexity of text planning or the recursive nature of writing. Instead, the writing process was often characterized as a uniform and definable series of steps that, if followed, produced successful texts.

Despite frequent misinterpretations, writing-process studies still resulted in revolutionary changes in the teaching of ESL, as they did in first language writing. The idea that students should draft papers (and that these drafts should be peer critiqued); that they should revise completely, making major changes in the organization and content of the paper; that they should share their work with their peers for comment; and that they should not edit for minor errors until they had completed the final draft—this freed us all from requiring a perfect product from students the first time they attempted to write a paper, something that had been expected under the older "current-traditional" approaches as advocated by Bander and many others. In many ways, my students were now more comfortable—and they enjoyed reflecting upon their writing processes as they proceeded through the course. They were also more comfortable because there was a class structure—and because they were required to edit and talk about grammatical structures, activities that had been ignored in some expressivist classrooms.

Despite its remarkable contributions to our discipline, the writing-process focus in the classroom presented some problems for ESL students in particular. They did not develop sensitivity to various genres, since the "English class" essay was, and continues to be, the most common writing assignment in process classes. They also didn't develop insights into the ways in which a variety of audiences outside of the classroom might respond to what they wrote. As a result, colleagues across campus informed my department that "even though they've completed your classes, your students don't know how to write." What they meant, of course, is that our students didn't know how to write *for them.*

There is a related problem that our ESL students face: they are so far away from the target university culture that they need much more assistance than is provided by the writing-process approach, that is, specific guidance in the structures and grammars of different types of texts. So, though we all saw "process" as a great advance for teaching, I continued in my quest for an ESL writing curriculum that would be more enabling and useful for ESL students.

Changing Castes—and Becoming a Journal Editor

OK, so the children were grown and had flown the coop (after we spent a year in China, where I had a Fulbright grant, training EFL teachers to teach writing), and I went after a high-caste position: a tenure-track appointment in linguistics and rhetoric and writing studies. This change of caste made me more confident to leave behind some of the textbooks and think more independently about pedagogy. The means was that I became coeditor, with John Swales, of the international journal *English for Specific Purposes,* which provided me with access to John's thinking—an extraordinary mind—and the opportunity to review ESP work that was being carried out throughout the world.

I began in earnest to be a journal editor. Undoubtedly, this experience of reading and reviewing colleagues' manuscripts has assisted me in becoming a more mature ESL teacher and teacher trainer. To that end, I have also had some remarkable opportunities to write for different audiences at San Diego State—for example, to revise and promote the proposal for the Department of Rhetoric and Writing Studies and to design and propose an "adjunct model" of instruction for a first-year learning-communities program, initially targeted for students requiring "remediation," all of whom are ESL or Generation 1.5. (See Johns, 1997, 2001b, for program descriptions; see Harklau, Losey, & Siegal, 1999; for a discussion of U.S.-educated immigrant students who still need ESL instruction—referred to as "Generation 1.5.")

The freedom from the acrimony of the English Department faculty (for your reading pleasure, consult, e.g., Russo's *The Straight Man* [1998]) and the chance to work on the adjunct program provided opportunities my colleagues and I had never dreamt of.[4] Because our adjunct-program links involve disciplines across the curriculum (e.g., biology, sociology, political science, anthropology, Africana and Chicano/a studies), we have been able to research the disciplinary practices and genres valued in many contexts.

Always keeping in mind the importance of the evolving nature of genres and disciplinary practices, we have designed writing courses at a number of proficiency levels that are "generative," that is, built around a writing portfolio of different pedagogical genres, such as summaries/abstracts, texts written from sources, process essays, and reviews/critiques. At the same time, we encourage students to become researchers into the texts required in their various courses and into ways to negotiate these texts so that they can write papers that suit their needs but yet remain appropriate to the assignment. In some cases, the writing faculty are working with faculty from other disciplines to conduct research or co-construct syllabi or assignments (see Johns, 1997).

So Where Does This End, at Least for Now?

This is a long-winded story of a person who began with a simple, though effective, approach to basic literacy (LEA) and moved on to increasingly complex approaches—but has realized that what we really need to do in the finite period of time we have with our students is genre analysis. That is, we must provide the kind of instruction that encourages them to be confident and observant in the many contexts in which they read and write. Just as we cannot teach them the entire English language, we cannot teach them all they need to know about muses, processes, and genres. So we must encourage them to be crafty, analytical, and self-critical, but sufficiently confident to approach new writing situations with a metalanguage with which to ask questions and study contexts.

What have I learned, then, from these experiences of wandering and experimentation? That we composition teachers need to take a careful look at our theories of learning and writing, at our students, and at the experiences with literacy they bring to the classroom, as well as at what students will need after they leave us. We need to relate theory to practice and to relate our ways of teaching to the needs of students. And, in particular, we need to consider what we can do, or encourage, in the classroom that will enable students to develop a useful awareness of the remarkable textual worlds all around them.

What Are the Goals of a Genre-Based Class?

Almost 40 years of composition teaching have convinced me that the most effective approaches are the ones that acknowledge the complexity of the writing process as both cognitive and social—and that assist students in researching various literacy situations and genres. Thus, I argue that our students need to work on these goals:

- To know themselves as writers and know some of the characteristics of their approaches to producing written texts. To do this, they need to consider:

  — The writing processes they use to produce texts under a variety of timed and untimed situations. (So, e.g., we ask them to reflect upon how they approach the writing of an out-of-class assignment vs. how they approach writing for a timed examination.)
  — The roles they can and will take as writers in the world and what these roles mean for the texts they produce. (So, they need to take on different roles in the classroom as they write their texts: as experts, students, requesters, arguers.)

- To analyze the contexts in which they write. To do this, they need to

  — Identify the socially constructed name of the genre in which they will write (critique, book review) and attempt to find text models for analysis or obtain adequate directions for writing.
  — Identify the conventional (reoccurring and stereotypical) features of a genre. (These include the ways in which the texts from the genre are organized, the appropriate content, and the standard grammar and vocabulary.)
  — Consider how their ideas of a genre can or should be revised for the particular context in which it is being written. (As we know, not all research papers are alike—nor are all lab reports.)

- To consider strategies for understanding, evaluating, and adapting a genre for a specific audience. To do this, they need to:

— Study the audience's values, needs, and interests (see especially Coe, 2001).
— Come to terms with the power relationships between writer and audience—and decide whether these can be negotiated (see, e.g., Benesch, 2000).

- To develop ways to make a text the writer's own—yet successful within its context. To do this, students need to:

— Design arguments that are supported and true to the writer's own beliefs and values.
— Make their own views both clear and persuasive.

So where am I then in this 40-year story—and where are all of us as teachers of ESL/EFL? Are we providing writing alternatives to students, opportunities for them to examine and attempt texts from a number of genres? Are we considering audience, context, and the writer's role—as well as the text itself? After all these years, I still find myself overwhelmed by the complexities of teaching and learning second language literacies, yet I think that, in my genre-based approach to inquiry, I'm much closer to the answers than I once was . . . and so are my students.

Notes

1. They chose to mold themselves, I'm happy to report.
2. See my story about Luc's frustrations (Johns, 1991).
3. Paul Prior (2001), one of the most astute of our composition studies colleagues, makes an argument for voice that is much more appealing: "voice is simultaneously personal and social because discourse is understood as fundamentally historical, situated, and indexical" (p. 55).
4. Initially, the California State University (CSU) English Council disapproved of the adjunct model. However, after our campus was recognized for its model English for Academic Purposes program, other CSU campuses began to develop similar programs themselves.

References

Bander, R. G. (1971). *American English rhetoric.* New York: Holt, Rinehart, Winston.

Benesch, S. (2000). *Critical English for academic purposes: Theory, politics, and practice.* Mahwah, NJ: Lawrence Erlbaum Associates.

Coe, R. M. (2001). The new rhetoric of genre: Writing political briefs. In A. M. Johns (Ed.), *Genre in the classroom: Multiple perspectives* (pp. 197–209). Mahwah, NJ: Lawrence Erlbaum Associates.

Dixon, C. N., & Nessel, D. (1983). *Language experience approach to reading (and writing): LEA for ESL.* Hayward, CA: Alemany Press.

Dudley-Evans, T., & St. John, M. J. (1998). *Developments in English for specific purposes: A multi-disciplinary approach.* Cambridge: Cambridge University Press.

Harklau, L., Losey, K. M., & Siegal, M. (Eds.) (1999). *Generation 1.5 meets college composition.* Mahwah, NJ: Lawrence Erlbaum Associates.

Johns, A. M. (1990). L1 composition theories: Implications for developing theories of L2 composition. In B. Kroll (Ed.), *Second language writing: Research insights for the classroom* (pp. 24–36). New York: Cambridge University Press.

Johns, A. M. (1991). Interpreting an English competency examination: The frustrations of an ESL science student. *Written Communication, 8,* 379–401.

Johns, A. M. (1997). *Text, role, and context: Developing academic literacies.* New York: Cambridge University Press.

Johns, A. M. (2001a). ESL students and WAC programs: Varied populations and diverse needs. In S. McLeod, E. Miraglia, M. Soven, & C. Thaiss (Eds.), *WAC for the new millennium: Strategies for continuing writing-across-the-curriculum programs,* (pp. 141–164). Urbana, IL: National Council of Teachers of English.

Johns, A. M. (2001b). An interdisciplinary, interinstitutional learning communities program: Student involvement and student success. In I. Leki (Ed.), *Academic writing programs* (pp. 61–72). Alexandria, VA: TESOL.

Little, S., & Rose, S. (1994). A home of our own: Establishing a department of rhetoric and writing studies at San Diego State University. *WPA: Writing Program Administration, 18 (1–2),* 16–28.

Prior, P. (2001). Voices in text, mind, and society: Sociohistoric accounts of discourse acquisition and use. *Journal of Second Language Writing* (Special Issue *Voice in L2 writing.* Guest edited by A. Hirvela & D. Belcher), *10,* 55–81.

Raimes, A. (1985). What unskilled writers do as they write: A classroom study. *TESOL Quarterly, 19,* 229–258.

Russo, R. (1998). *The straight man.* New York: Vintage Books.

Silva, T. (1990). Second language composition instruction: Developments, issues, and directions in ESL. In B. Kroll (Ed.), *Second language writing: Research insights for the classroom* (pp. 11–23). New York: Cambridge University Press.

Spack, R. (1984). Invention strategies and the ESL college composition student. *TESOL Quarterly, 18,* 649–670.

Swales, J. M. (1988). *Episodes in ESP: A source and reference book on the development of English for science and technology.* New York: Prentice-Hall.

Zamel, V. (1982). Writing: The process of discovering meaning. *TESOL Quarterly, 16,* 195–209.

Zamel, V. (1983). The composing processes of advanced ESL students: Six case studies. *TESOL Quarterly, 17,* 165–187.

> *When Alister Cumming started teaching ESL in his early twenties,*
> *nearly every day as he strolled to his classes through the crowded*
> *hallways of Vancouver Community College, someone (thinking*
> *he must be a student) would direct him to the student lounge.*
> *Was it the expression of anxiety or helplessness on his face? Or*
> *was it the shoulder-length hair and curly beard? At any rate,*
> *nobody seems to make that mistake anymore, and this is pre-*
> *sumably not because his hair and beard are now closely*
> *cropped.*

If I Had Known
Twelve Things . . .

Alister Cumming

Ontario Institute for Studies in Education/University of Toronto

The utter complexity is what strikes me, if I reflect on the things that I know now that I wish I had known when I started teaching ESL writing. Indeed, the thought makes me recall the deep, moaning voice of Marlon Brando as General Kurtz in the film *Apocalypse Now* (echoing Conrad's *Heart of Darkness*): ". . . the horror, the horror. . . ." An overstatement for sure, but a reflection of the perception of bewildering complexity that I have come to understand ESL writing instruction to involve as my career has moved over the past two decades from teaching ESL writing, to coordinating programs in which this has been a central component, to conducting research on this topic and helping graduate students and others (such as educational agencies and other scholars) conduct their research on various issues related to literacy in second languages. Throughout this work, my guiding views have mixed (*a*) a sense of the complexity of the factors associated with teaching and learning ESL writing and (consequently) (*b*) the need for systematic inquiry to establish reliable information to help understand this complexity and know how to act on it in a principled manner.

As I reflect on what I have learned, I think of (1) six "principles" that I came to believe in through my teaching practice and discussions with those colleagues who acted as mentors (principles that I continue to adhere to and believe are valuable); and (2) six "practices" that I employed in my initial years of teaching and that I still hear others advocating but about which I now have serious doubts, or at least I consider them to be much more complex and poorly understood than discussions about teaching ESL writing might lead us to believe.

Both categories, of principles and practices, represent things I didn't know when I started teaching in this area, perhaps because they were not emphasized in my initial teacher education (where the one class period on ESL writing consisted solely of a discussion of Robert Kaplan's [1966] ideas about contrastive rhetoric) or were not considered very critically among the colleagues with whom I first worked. Or perhaps they were overshadowed by my own initial concerns for what to teach and how to teach it. But they have become enduring concerns in my work and indeed in the work of many other people (represented in the present collection and elsewhere).

Following, I describe them from the viewpoint of teaching, but they extend as well to curriculum organization and educational policy. I think they apply to the classes of graduate students with whom I now work, particularly in my helping them as first and second language writers of term papers and theses. And they apply as well to the ESL students in courses with whom I worked in my initial decade of teaching—in the contexts of evening courses in colleges, summer intensive programs, or the first year of university.

Teaching ESL by Coincidence

Before I describe these principles, let me tell you a bit about the situations in which I first taught. I entered this field as much by coincidence and particular life circumstances as anything else, not unlike many of my colleagues, including several represented in this volume: Ann M. Johns, Barbara Kroll, Joy Reid, Tony Silva. In the final semester of studies for my bachelor's degree, I couldn't make up my mind whether I should finish the degree with a major in biology (with its scientific rigor and open window on nature) or in English literature (with its concerns for people, words, and cultures). I happened to take a course in linguistics because I had been told it would be a requirement for further studies in English.

A tall lanky fellow named Bill Gibson often sat beside me at the back of these classes. One day he turned to me, suggesting that if, after this linguistics course, I took a couple more courses in the summer about teaching ESL, I could work at the local college (as his wife did) teaching English to immigrants for 16 dollars an hour, then an impressive sum, even in Canadian dollars. So I did—realizing that this was far more money and status than I had in my part-time job as an assistant in an ecologist's lab. Within weeks of starting the TESL courses, all of us students in the class were recruited to teach six hours a day to an unexpected influx of immigrants and refugees to Vancouver. Bill went on to fame as a science fiction writer and icon of "cyberpunk," but of course that is his story . . .

I scrambled and floundered through my first year of teaching. During the evenings I was studying how a person is supposed to teach ESL at the same time as I was doing it, unbelievably, for six hours a day, five days a week. But I enjoyed the challenges of creating new activities every day, of interacting with people from truly diverse parts of the world, and of learning how to organize them to make the most of their English studies and resettlement in Canada. Recognizing that I was just learning the profession, nobody asked me to teach writing (which was allocated to the experienced, better-educated instructors). Writing seldom featured as much of an activity in those classes, because the students tended to want to learn spoken English so they could find jobs and function in their communities.

After this initial "survival" phase, I applied to work in the local university's intensive English programs, where I joined colleagues who worked closely in teams, developing an inno-vative curriculum aimed at giving the best-quality experience of learning English to short-term visitors to Vancouver, mostly from Quebec or Japan. That context helped focus me on the principles I later describe, as I was prompted to exam-ine critically my own teaching alongside others with whom I team-taught, while we jointly created an innovative curricu-lum, based not on grammar but on the experiences of the learners, the features of natural discourse, and the local cul-ture and media our students sought to appreciate. I had no awareness at the time that we were, like many others in the 1970s around the world, establishing the value of commu-nicative orientations to language teaching and learning. (See Linda Lonon Blanton's chapter for more about this history.)

It was several more years before I got into teaching ESL composition, first while doing a master's degree in TESL, then over the subsequent decade, as I moved to universities in Vancouver, Montreal, Ottawa, and Toronto. The master's degree seemed to make people think I should know more than the average ESL instructor about writing, though my own interests arose mainly as a concern for the qualities of peo-ple's expression, patterns of organization and words, and the freedom I had to juggle my own time (that is, to spend it responding to papers, on my own, rather than in classrooms teaching spoken English).

The people-oriented, interactional skills I had learned

while teaching extensive hours of intensive English served me well to animate the composition classrooms. But teaching writing presented a new set of challenges: how to get students through the final, standard exams (then, later in my career, how to design such assessments so that they reflected what I thought important for students to display); how to respond to students' writing so that they actually improved it; and how to capitalize on the diversity of interests and fields of knowledge that students from across the university possessed. I don't believe there were any particular epiphanies in my learning how to teach ESL composition but rather a gradual progression of experiences that broadened and deepened, from place to place and course to course, my conception of the complexities not just of writing but also of English, learning, and teaching.

Learning from My Teaching Practices

From my years of teaching, I can extract a set of principles that I believe sum up valuable ideas to guide writing teachers in a variety of situations. These are summed up here, and I will discuss each in turn.

Key Principles to Guide Writing Teachers
1. Assign purposeful, relevant writing tasks
2. Promote student contact with members of the TL (target language) community
3. Foster relationship building among students
4. Encourage students to take control of their own learning
5. Allow students sufficient time to achieve curriculum goals
6. Limit and focus teacher talk in the classroom

A major principle that I developed through teaching practice is that of the value of purposeful, relevant writing tasks. To learn to write meaningfully in a second language, people need to write about things that are important to them, be they the genres of writing they use in their academic courses or jobs or the topics that appeal to their personal senses of identity or self-expression. To be perceived as purposeful and to set a motivating context for learning, writing tasks have to derive from the genuine interests and perceived communication needs of the people who execute them. Conversely, treating writing tasks simply as exercises done for their own sake doesn't help to foster much worthwhile learning.

A second principle is that of promoting contact with key members of the TL discourse community. Having students interview professors, native-speaking friends, or interesting personalities who represent the TL population—then write about them and to them—helps students become members of that discourse community and orient their writing and language learning toward it. Although particularly vital in academic and professional settings, this cultural contact is important also for students on brief sojourns to countries where the language being learned is spoken and for students with email or written access to people in places where the language is used.

A third principle is that of fostering group support and relationship building among students in classes. Classrooms are social communities: Students can ably assist one another to learn in diverse ways, form partnerships that help to promote a communal interest in literate activity, and respond critically to each other's writing. Instruction can be organized to foster these relations and this cultural ambience productively, or it can denigrate these possibilities.

A fourth principle is to encourage students to develop control over their own learning processes. Learning to write in a second language is something that students have to take ownership of for themselves. It should not remain an abstract, mysterious process achieved by others or described by a teacher or textbook. To do this, students need to identify manageable goals for their own learning, analyzing what they know and don't know, finding out how others have made their achievements in this area, and monitoring the achievements they progressively make themselves.

A related, fifth principle is that of allowing students sufficient time and supportive conditions to practice and improve their ESL writing in substantive and clearly defined ways. The major mistake I have seen curriculum policies make in respect to ESL writing is that of expecting too much to happen in too short a time and not being very clear about what these achievements should be. In my experience, students can achieve a few distinct, worthwhile goals over the period of one semester, if their learning activities are focused distinctly on these. But writing is so complex and multifaceted that we should not expect much more than this to emerge in one course. Unfortunately, university or college policies tend to expect major, global developments among students in the period of one course, but they seldom say precisely what these developments should be. Systematic research and theories on student achievement in ESL writing are sadly lacking, to the detriment and confusion of all our work.

A sixth principle I have tried to develop while teaching is that of restricting but focusing my own talk in classes so as to permit the other principles to operate. I became aware in my initial years of teaching that if I talked too much, and thus dominated the arena of classroom activities with my own preoccupations as an instructor, then the focus on learners, learning, and emerging cultural communities described earlier could hardly develop. I perceived this first as a need to take the focus of attention off of myself (as instructor) and put it onto the students (as learners), organizing activities in my classrooms so as to achieve learning primarily, not just teaching. Gradually, I have come to see how I can focus my spoken and written interactions with students to help them better achieve their purposes. But I am still learning how to do this.

Cultivating Caution

Having enumerated the six principles, I see that they look slightly Deweyian in their humanistic orientation and in their vagueness. (These are characteristics of John Dewey's writing about education that have always both fascinated and exasperated me; see, e.g., Dewey, 1963.) So I feel the need to temper them with a comparable set of cautions concerning teaching practices that I have come to question. Following, some of the common practices that I believe need to be examined more fully are listed. Even though many in the field continue to advocate each of these notions, my years of teaching have taught me that the issues are more complex than might at first be apparent.

Common Practices Needing to Be Questioned

1. Believing there is a single solution to the problem of teaching ESL writing
2. Using published texts as writing models
3. Requiring only TL use in the L2 classroom
4. Dwelling on error correction
5. Making assumptions about language learners as a whole
6. Separating writing into component skills

In questioning these practices, I do not mean to suggest that I know they are wrong in any absolute sense but rather to state that I question them because my experiences with them have been mixed and the knowledge available about them from research is limited. In short, I just don't know, so I have come to be wary about them.

Indeed, the first of these is to distrust people who say they have a single, simple, straightforward solution to the difficult problems of teaching ESL writing. (This includes myself in the earlier paragraphs.) ESL writing is complex, involving numerous interrelated factors related to people's differing backgrounds, life experiences with literacy, ages, sociolinguistic situations, and purposes for writing and learning. These vary greatly from situation to situation, and even person to person, defying simple, general solutions to pedagogical problems. This complexity is not insurmountable; people learn to write in second languages everyday. But it is not easily explained or orchestrated in a classroom. And it does not happen in a simple, uniform manner.

Second, I question the value of text models alone in helping people to learn to write in a second language. Although certainly valuable, and probably even necessary, for learning to write in a second language, models of text structures (be they grammatical or rhetorical) are but one kind of model that students need to learn from. Equally important are psychological models (of the processes of thinking and identity formation that people use or develop when they compose) and sociocultural models (of the interactions between writers and readers and of the discourse communities within which they function, as Ann M. Johns writes about in her tale). When I started teaching ESL writing in the early 1970s, pedagogical practices centered almost exclusively on learners analyzing and rehearsing grammatical and rhetorical paradigms, a perspective that I (and much research since then) have come to see as limited and limiting when one considers additional, complementary dimensions of composing, language processing, and learning (see Cumming, 1998).

A third practice I now question is the exclusive use of the TL in second language classrooms. Second language students use their mother tongues and their existing knowledge (situated in these languages) in important, distinct ways while they compose. These occur mentally (e.g., in searching for the best words to convey their intended expressions), linguistically (e.g., in contrasting rhetorical expectations in one language against another), and culturally (e.g., in analyzing one's writing in cooperation with peers and other knowledge resources, and in building cultural solidarity). It is more productive, I have come to believe, to encourage second language learners to use these cross-linguistic resources effectively when they write, rather than to try to "indoctrinate" learners into using English alone (or any other TL), as suggested by many educational policies.

The fourth practice I wonder about seriously is that of error correction. I suspect this may be useful in certain ways, such as helping students to analyze and talk about their writing in a second language, but we know so little about these things at present, or how to do them purposefully, that I fear that teachers' error corrections may in many instances hinder rather than help the development of second language writing. Given the pervasive tendency of instructors to attempt to correct second language writing, this is a topic on which we need much more research. This research needs to recognize the complexity of issues involved. Plus, it needs to acknowledge the diverse ways in which errors appear and study the following: how errors can interact with learning processes, curricula, and sociolinguistic contexts; how they are addressed by teachers; and how they may be perceived and acted on differently by learners and by particular readers of students' texts.

As an instructor, I find myself asking: What will this student do with the correction I make to this piece of writing? What value does it serve? To be sure, many language learners ask for corrections of their writing, but I have found that more students respond positively, and motivate themselves to improve their writing (in ways that I could never have anticipated), when the responses I give to their texts try concertedly to value their ideas and purposes as well as to encourage their academic and intellectual development, rather than just to edit mistakes.

The fifth practice I now question is that of making simple assumptions about language learners. This is not just a matter of avoiding cultural stereotypes, as important as that is, or querying the prescriptions of simple versions of contrastive analysis. More crucially, people who are learning to write in a second language vary so greatly in their backgrounds, situations, personalities, interests, needs, and aims that it is difficult, and I think even dangerous, to attempt to predict in advance what they might or should need to learn to do.

In teaching writing, instructors need to investigate their students' individual situations carefully and then use this information to help them with learning activities, while appreciating and building upon their uniqueness. This process extends beyond assessing students' needs at the start of a course (though it might usefully start there) and should include ways of assisting individuals through the duration and over the range of their learning, recognizing that individuals learn in diverse ways and that their learning interacts progressively with their achievements and circumstances outside of classrooms.

The sixth practice that I now seriously question (and have alluded to in several places earlier) is the use of many kinds of "exercises" that separate writing into componential skills. Such exercises inevitably diminish the task of writing into subactivities that are seldom integral to the activity overall, eliminating its complexity and personal and cultural significance. Hence they are of limited value in promoting learning that aims to address this complexity and significance. Perhaps because the concept of "exercise" is the basis for conventional textbook instruction, designed to be administered to masses of students in a uniform way, it runs counter to most of the principles I have come to believe in as vital, based on my personal classroom experiences with particular people. Moreover, the concept of "exercise" can lead teachers (like myself in the initial years of teaching) into seemingly straightforward (but limited) solutions to very complex issues.

Not the End But the Beginning

Considering all twelve of these principles and practices together, each presents for me, not a final synopsis of the state of my current knowledge, but rather a topic that needs to be evaluated and better understood through future research, analyses of teaching practices, enhanced frameworks for curriculum organization, and improvements to teacher education and professional development. Despite the complexities they entail, I am optimistic that they can be better understood and better acted upon.

References

Cumming, A. (1998). Theoretical perspectives on writing. *Annual Review of Applied Linguistics, 18,* 207–224.

Dewey, J. (1963). *Experience and education.* New York: Collier Books.

Kaplan, R. B. (1966). Cultural thought patterns in intercultural education. *Language Learning, 16,* 1–20.

Unlike some of her colleagues in this collection, Linda Lonon Blanton didn't grow up wanting to become a teacher. In fact, she swore she wouldn't be the one thing women in her family were expected to be. She was, however, never opposed to the enterprise of education: in grade school, she earned pocket money from her classmates by surreptitiously doing their homework for them. Still earning an income, albeit modest, from the enterprise of education, she is now content that the one sure way to remain a life-long learner (and do her own homework) is to teach.

As I Was Saying to Leonard Bloomfield
A Personalized History of ESL/Writing

Linda Lonon Blanton
University of New Orleans

Dr. Bloomfield . . . Call you Leonard? No, really, I couldn't. . . . You know, I have the feeling you might be surprised by the half century of development that spread, like ripples in a pond, from your shaping of Anglo-American linguistics. I say "your," because, really, you know, you changed the face of the field. From philology as philosophy to linguistics as its own discipline. From a study of the etymology of written words to the structure of spoken form. The evolution was phenomenal. . . . Chomsky? Silly me. Of course, you wouldn't have heard of him. Got a minute?

When I first taught English to non-native speakers, I had never heard of Leonard Bloomfield. (*Sorry, Dr. Bloomfield.*) I had no knowledge of theory nor consciousness of pedagogy. And I didn't teach writing because no one did. In reaction to the dark ages of teaching language *as* translation, the new age framed language as something to be spoken. This was the 1960s.

I start in the 1960s with my ESL story, not only because that's where *I* began but also because it allows me to come "behind" the other tales in the collection and frame them historically. To do this, I need to tell the *whole* story, the story of greater ESL, in order to situate L2 writing in its midst. In so doing, I hope to shed light for new ESL teachers on what the field was like before they came along. As for me, a veteran of the classroom, telling my tale enables me to understand bet ter how it was and is. (*On second thought, Dr. B., this'll take more than a minute. But I bet you knew that anyway. Bear with me.*)

Applying Linguistics

"Modern" language lessons, in the 1960s, you see, were designed for the purpose of promoting oral proficiency. With newly evolved structural linguistics as ESL's theoretical base (ESL representing the "applied" proving ground of linguistic knowledge), the instructional goal was for students to speak the way educated native speakers actually speak, not to read or write the language. And the way educated native speakers actually speak—that is, their use of the very syntactic and phonological elements taught in ESL classes—was discerned from recorded natural speech, through linguists' analysis of what they call a "corpus." (Not a dead body, a corpus is the sum of a researcher's live data.)

The scientific method of "discovering" the results—that is, the language patterns themselves, revealed dispassionately through an analysis of frequency of occurrence—was a point of pride among Bloomfieldian linguists, since prior notions of English structure were based on how nineteenth- (and even some eighteenth-) century grammarians thought the language *should* be, as opposed to its actual twentieth-century use. And some grammarians thought English should "behave" like Latin, not like the Germanic language it is, and wrote their rules accordingly. All this, though, I learned later in graduate school.

(*This, Dr. B., is what I was getting at earlier.*) The beginnings of ESL cannot be understood without knowledge of the thinking of American linguist Leonard Bloomfield (1914/1983, 1933) and the evolution of structural linguistics. Structural linguists studied the phenomenon of language *as* structure—breath and tongue and vocal chords working together to form what an English speaker "hears" as an English language sound (phonological structure); sounds working together systematically to form meaningful bits an English speaker hears as, say, plural *sofas* (with *ZZZ*) and not singular *sofa* (morphological structure); combinations of sounds a speaker perceives as words strung together in one order but not another to end up with, say, *Mary kissed John* and not *John kissed Mary* (syntactic structure); and so on, through semantic and pragmatic structures—like little Chinese boxes fit into larger ones to constitute what we think of as full-blown language. For a good 50 years, Bloomfield's students and, in turn, their students (and their students' students) held sway, creating linguistic atlases, documenting varieties of American English, analyzing native languages, and developing analytic tools for research in phonetics, phonology, morphology, syntax, and semantics. (*We owe you, Dr. B.*)

Kenneth Pike, who established the scientific study of phonetics and phonemics; George Trager and Henry Lee Smith, who codified the phoneme as the underlying operational unit in speech analysis; Hans Kurath, Raven McDavid, and Albert Marckwardt, who established dialect geography as a science; C. C. Fries, who pioneered the scientific collection of grammatical data—these are the Bloomfieldians whose work I later cut my linguistics teeth on. When I was in graduate school, I had the chance to actually meet some of them at conferences through my mentor Alva (Al) Davis, a dialectologist. Awed, I thought of them as the grand old men of American linguistics, not realizing until later that they were actually of several different generations and in some cases were students of each other. (Al Davis, for example, was Marckwardt's student.)

The influence of structural linguistics was later eclipsed by the rise of Chomskyian linguistics—of what Noam Chomsky's students initially called "transformational grammar," which Chomsky himself called "Cartesian linguistics." The impact of this new school of linguistics, with its attempts to get to the bottom of what makes human language unique, began to be felt in the early 1970s, although Chomsky's *Syntactic Structures,* which started the ball rolling, was published in 1957. Little happens overnight. (*I'll say more about Chomsky later, Dr. B.*)

Forays into Textbook Land

But to return to my story. After completing my undergraduate degree in British literature, I flew off to Peace Corps training at Princeton University in the summer of 1964, having been told that my posting was Tunisia, to teach EFL. (I had never heard of EFL *or* Tunisia.) Placed in my hands were all of the English language teaching textbooks then currently available.

For teaching grammar—remember, life was simple—there was the *Green Book.* For pronunciation, the *Yellow Book.* For stress and intonation, the *Red Book,* with fold-out picture charts. They had real titles, of course: the green one was *English Sentence Patterns* (Lado & Fries, 1958; subsequently revised by Krohn [1972]); the red was *English Pattern Practices* (Lado & Fries, 1943); and the yellow was *English Pronunciation* (Lado & Fries, 1954). But we referred to them as if colors were their titles and called them collectively the "Michigan materials," since they were written by faculty at the first-in-the-nation intensive ESL program, the English Language Institute (ELI) at the University of Michigan. (Later, the ELI faculty came out with the *Blue Book* [*Vocabulary in Context* (Franklin, Meikle, & Strain, 1967)], so vocabulary was added to ESL teaching, but still no one taught writing or reading.)

Peace Corps trainers also gave everyone in my group *Teaching and Learning English as a Foreign Language* (1945), by C. C. Fries, a student of Bloomfield and the father of the Michigan ELI. (Later, I also thought of Fries as the father of applied linguistics, since, to my mind, he was *the* Bloomfieldian most interested in applying structural linguistic knowledge to English language instruction.)

I'm ashamed to admit that, before Peace Corps training, I had never given much thought to English as a language, or as something to be learned or taught. But armed with my green, yellow, and red textbooks, and with the Fries volume in hand, I voyaged off to the Bourguiba Institute (now part of the University of Tunis), where I spent two years learning about teaching English as a language by experimenting on adult students. All of these EFL/ESL teaching materials—and I basically had everything on the market—occupied no more than a bookshelf. Maybe half a shelf. (And, by the way, no distinction was made between English as a "foreign language" and as a "second language." It was all foreign.)

Later, in a decided theoretical break from earlier materials but still under the auspices of Michigan's ELI, Mary Lawrence published *Writing as a Thinking Process* (1972), which set me to thinking more about the complexities of writing. Even so, the beginning ESL levels still had no writing books available, nor did my intensive ESL program have any beginning or intermediate classes devoted to writing. (By then I was teaching at the Central Y Community College in Chicago, in an ESL program largely staffed by returned Peace

Corps volunteers, who were, in the 1960s and early 1970s, about the only hires around with prior English language teaching experience.)

At Central Y, I surreptitiously turned one of my beginning grammar classes into a composition class and wrote materials to keep up with my students. I remember well the textbook I was supposed to use: Costinett's *Structure Graded Readings in English* (1970), which I didn't use because I wanted students to write. The book, for those too young to have been there, was basically a series of paragraphs—of unnatural sentences strung together—followed by grammar exercises.

By keeping up with students and refining my mimeographed lessons by trial and error, I basically had, after a semester or two, a textbook-length manuscript. (This is often how textbooks get written—quite unintentionally—as Joy Reid also recounts in her tale.) But tiring of copying the lessons for classes, and for colleagues who'd heard I had a set of materials to "lend," I approached a publisher. The response was, "You can't teach writing at the beginning levels. ESL students have to *speak* English before they can write it." As if ESL college students weren't already literate in other languages before they enrolled in ESL. (Granted, this view doesn't account for "Generation 1.5," a newer population of USA-educated ESL students, but that's a later story.)

One publisher rejected my materials because they would "not compete well against Mary Lawrence's book." (Mine were written for the opposite end of the proficiency spectrum.) He couldn't understand that I was writing for the "be-gin-ning" level, even when I said it slowly. For a time, I gave up trying to publish the materials and kept cranking out smelly, purple, mimeographed sheets for students and colleagues. Later, these materials became the "anchor" in a four-book series published by Newbury House (Blanton, 1977, 1978), which, just prior to that, had completed a new master plan calling for low-level composition textbooks. (Blessed with a long life, the series has just come out in its third edition: Blanton, 2001a.) I guess then I was ahead of my time.

Inside and Outside the Box

How can I say this without seeming smug, which honestly is not how I feel? Most teachers in those days thought even of *adult* ESL student writers as blank slates. Really, the field evidenced little awareness of how literacy, once acquired, transfers from one language to another. We had no sense of how to build on a base of literacy, already established, to help students compose in English. Except for the commonplace sense of the absence of literacy—that is, illiteracy—as an unfamiliarity with written symbols, we (at least I) hadn't really thought about literacy, period, let alone about literacy as a way of being in the world, as a multitude of acquired behaviors, as central to the complex and complicated role of reading and writing in one's life. In that aspect of teaching, I was most assuredly not ahead of my time but firmly rooted in it.

I began teaching writing, though, before we understood that ESL college students can *be* writers—in fact, might already have become proficient writers of their home languages—even before they become fluent and fluid writers of English, their second or third or fourth language. Before we learned that ESL students become more fluent writers of English by writing English before they are fluent. That the writing process itself promotes fluency and greater proficiency.

Granted, there is much we didn't know, and we did some things that, looking back, seem pretty silly, but we were starting from scratch and feeling our way along. The field was new. (*You know about the absence of guideposts, don't you, Dr. B.?*) There were almost no graduate programs to provide training. Besides, linguistics and its applications, along with other fields, were caught in the grips of behaviorist psychology. And our understanding of learning—language learning or learning of *any* sort—was that imitation and repetition were the behaviors that enabled simulation of the model and, after enough perfect repetition, ultimate inculcation. Listen, repeat, substitute, transform. Bingo, mission accomplished. On to the next pattern. (*Did you have a premonition of this, Dr. B.? . . . I didn't think so.*)

As we learned—and saw that students stood in the hallway, on break, and spoke imperfectly to each other the patterns drilled perfectly in class—we experimented outside the box. And we began asking questions like these: If the audio-lingual method is too drill oriented, then what about a communicative approach? Shouldn't one want to say some*thing* to some*one*? Don't the purpose and context for language use matter?

Christina Paulston and Mary Bruder at the University of Pittsburgh did get us thinking a bit about language *as* communication, about ignoring some learner errors, and about not just drilling for grammar's sake. The irony—that structural linguists built their knowledge of English by analyzing spoken language, that is, conversations in context, and we applied linguists were busy teaching language devoid of communicative purpose and context—is now painfully obvious. Trust me, it wasn't obvious then.

Paulston and Bruder's book *From Substitution to Substance* (1975), while still situated within an audio-lingual framework, does introduce meaning into the mix. Granted, it's meaning of a limited sort, but meaning nevertheless. We may feel embarrassed today to think about how radical these notions seemed then, but conceptual change is always revolutionary. (*No one knows that better than you, Dr. B.*)

Newly concerned with meaning, we talked about organizing materials along semantic lines, if indeed lessons seemed too grammar focused and meaning-less. In fact, the term *notional/functional* began appearing in textbook titles to signal this orientation. (See Coffey, 1983, for a later example.) Unlike traditional groupings according to syntactic and verb-tense categories (e.g., past progressives, adverbials of place, modals, conditionals), these state-of-the-art textbooks were organized around a speaker's purpose (e.g., greetings, apologies, compliments, requests, invitations). Yet, of course, the field was still constrained by behaviorist thinking (a grip that holds to this day), and the notions and functions were drilled as grammatical patterns, but the inclusion of semantic concerns *was* progress.

ESL Branches Out

We also began asking why, if some ESL students were training to become, say, nurses or air-traffic controllers, they were being served by the same generalized instructional materials as everyone else. Besides, who in the world speaks "general" English anyway? Within a context of awareness of language diversity, research on field-specific English got underway. The result was the outgrowth of English for Specific Purposes (ESP), an effort girded by insight and intelligence but, despite its abbreviation, devoid of crystal balls.

John Swales, whom I'd call—along with Mary Todd Trimble, Louis Trimble, and John Lackstrom—a "parent" of ESP, published at the time an L2 textbook on scientific English (Swales, 1971) that set me to thinking more about the relevance of ESL writing materials. Swales tied the language of the book to the context in which ESL learners might need to write and then let the specialized context determine the register and content of the lessons—quite an obvious thing to do, but something not thought about before. (See Trimble, Trimble, & Drobnic, 1978, for the beginnings of ESP.)

Published in Canada in 1971, Swales's *Writing Scientific English* didn't make it across the border—or into my hands, at least—until 1975. By that time I was back in ESL full swing after taking time away to complete a doctoral program in structural linguistics, with dissertation research in the mountains of Kentucky on the morphological structure of Appalachian English. On seeing Swales's book, I proposed to my community college colleagues—I had returned to my old job—that we offer an ESL course in scientific writing. The reaction was, "*We're* not science teachers," but I got approval and began designing such a course. (Curriculum design should, of course, come before materials development—or even before searching the market for a textbook—but in actuality it often works the other way. Here, the textbook provided me not only the materials for the course but also the idea for it.)

So, I initiated this new elective course in scientific writing in my community college ESL program in Chicago. Students loved the course and registered for it in droves. Their concerns about the articulation between ESL class work and just-around-the-corner college course demands were being addressed. Of course they loved it. Finally, a course they saw as relevant.

Considering Cognition

Another question we began asking was, if class time seemed teacher dominated, how to get students participating more? (Drilling didn't count as participation.) If passivity—if not brain-dead boredom—was slowing learning, how about using an approach called "total physical response" (TPR)? In 1982, James Asher, a psychologist at San Jose (California) State University, tendered the idea—revolutionary in language-teaching circles—that when learners matched physical movement to meaning, it aided them in internalizing language. Plus, if they waited until they were ready to speak (that is, they weren't pressed to speak prematurely), it would also lower their stress level and, as a result, improve their learning. *Stand up* (and they stood), *sit down* (and they sat), *walk to the window* (and they did). Classrooms turned active and joyful.

Did students feel *comfortable*? Did they feel *ready*? What odd questions. Who in the trenches had thought much about how L2 learners actually *felt*? I can't say I had. Well, I take that back—I had, in a certain way, but I hadn't actually thought about how students' feelings might affect their brain function, impacting the quantity and tempo of learning. With the arrival and widespread use of TPR, the paradigm really did shift— from behaviorism to cognitivism, a conceptual framework based on presumed links between affect and learning, between the brain and emotions. Chomskyian linguistics, meet ESL. (*You're wondering about the connection, Dr. B.? See if this makes sense.*)

While Chomsky's transformational grammar, based on Cartesian rationalism, has no overt ties to affect or emotion, it *is* cognitivist to its core, reflecting as it does "certain fundamental properties of the [human] mind" (Chomsky, 1966, p. 59). Chomsky's thinking went like this: Human language is biologically determined, with each of us born with the ability to "derive the structural regularities—its grammatical rules— of our native language from the utterances of parents and others around [us], and then to make use of the same regularities in the construction of utterances [we] have never heard before" (Lyons, 1970, p. 4). Since humans are born with brains that are, so to speak, wired for language, it is the linguistic environment that determines which "button" gets turned on to refine the elements in the brain into what we call, say, Arabic, Urdu, or English.

Even if Chomsky said his work was unrelated to language instruction and bore no application—I heard him say it myself—it cannot be coincidental that the ESL paradigm shifted to cognitive concerns in the decades just after transformational grammar gained dominance in theoretical linguistics. (Despite earlier attempts by structural linguists to quarantine linguistic theory to keep it "pure," theory was not hermetically sealed from practice. It leaked out and over.) (*Uh oh, I see it on your face, Dr. B. "Quarantine" is not how you'd put it.*)

The Impact of Cognitive Theory

As proof of the impact of ESL's shift to cognitive concerns, let me mention briefly the work of two second language educators, Stephen Krashen, of the University of Southern California, and Jim Cummins, of the Ontario Institute of Studies in Education/University of Toronto. Working from a base of cognitive theory, both began stirring up applied linguistics in the late 1970s and early 1980s. I discovered Krashen's work first.

Extrapolating from Chomsky's theory of child (first) language acquisition, Krashen analyzed second language environments to find commonality between the two. I was impressed. As I saw it, here was someone of *my* generation— and a fellow returned Peace Corps volunteer (Ethiopia) at that—actually saying powerful things about second language *learning* and not just talking about *teaching*. (See early Krashen, 1978, 1982). Finally, direct linkage between theory and practice to help answer some of my own questions.

Through Krashen's acquisition-learning distinction, I understood why I, earlier as a high-school and then as a college student, had not emerged from "foreign" language classrooms (first Spanish, then German) with any degree of fluency. With a sinking feeling in the pit of my stomach, it came over me, as I read Krashen, that while I had hoped (way back then) to gain some competence *in* those languages, I had instead learned *about* them. A methodology that taught me German and Spanish grammatical rules, and was compatible with class time spent conjugating verbs, had not enabled me to speak Spanish or German, even minimally. I understood why, on the contrary, I had become a fluent speaker of French during my Peace Corps days in then-French-speaking Tunisia, because with opportunities aplenty to struggle and often even succeed in "real" communication, the environment had been conducive to language *acquisition*. In other words, I had largely "picked up" French.

I also understood from Krashen's " input" theory why L2 students could be totally surrounded by language and *not* pick it up without a buddy/mentor to bring it down to their level and make it comprehensible, which turns it into fuel for the acquisition process. I understood why I could, say, listen to Chinese radio every day for the rest of my life and not become a speaker of Chinese. No wonder I had subconsciously known, during my first Peace Corps months in Tunisia, to hang around French-speaking *children* while trying my wings in French. Their simplified French was understandable to me. Besides, they didn't care if I got the grammar wrong or my accent was atrocious. They still talked to me as long as they could figure out what I was saying—all of which kept low my level of stress (that is, my *affective filter*, Krashen's term), allowing my brain to process the new language and progress.

And, from Krashen's research, I also began to understand why adult students (whether L2 *or* L1) who come to writing later, without early committed (positive) experience in reading and writing, do not respond well to school writing instruction. That writing at its core *is* literacy, a complex of behaviors that develops over time in text-rich, nurturing environments. That aspects of writing *can* improve through classroom instruction—that is, students can gain valuable experience and needed confidence under our tutelage—but that classrooms are often rocky and barren places for literacy to grow. Krashen's slim and largely unnoticed volume on writing (1984) helped make that clear to me. (See also Kroll, 1979, for related work using Krashen's framework.)

The question of whether Krashen's work meant we language teachers were out of business—*Weren't languages best picked up without formal classroom instruction?*—was pretty much answered by Krashen and Terrell's *Natural Approach* (1983), in which they showed how classrooms could become sites for learning *and* acquisition. They showed how content-rich lessons taught at a learner's intellectual level could still be language-simplified enough for the language of instruction itself to serve as comprehensible input.

The general effect of cognitive theory—and of Krashen's work and second language acquisition theory, in particular—was a spurt (in the 1980s) of classroom materials filled with subject-matter content and not just grammatical form. Now we understood it was the linguistic *environment*—that is, immersion in and engagement with meaningful, comprehensible language—that enabled language proficiency to grow. This was most noticeable in L2 composition classes, where lessons came to be joined by theme or topic—integrated, that is, by content—and reading and writing were now more likely to be linked. Students could connect to their own knowledge and experience by working in thematic units on, say, work and professions (Raimes, 1987) or friends and families (Blanton, 1988, 2001b), rather than "writing" disconnected strings of sentences to practice, say, the simple past tense. It may be unbelievable to new ESL teachers that it took a paradigmatic shift to get to that point, but it did. (*You're right, Dr. B. I am simplifying, but only somewhat.*)

More Impact of Cognitive Theory

While a shift in focus from teaching to learning (from behaviorism to cognitivism) *sounds* simple enough, it truly rearranged the landscape of language instruction. Take also the work of Jim Cummins. (See early Cummins, 1976, 1979,

1984.) As I see it, Cummins's work had less impact than Krashen's on second language composition (which is largely focused on adult learners), but only because Cummins' work focused then (and still does) on bilingual children. It is, however, no less important. I'll explain by way of telling what was helpful to me.

For one, I found that Cummins's work provided me with a clearer way of talking (and thinking) about the *difficulty* of language use, which is hard to grasp when you are already fluent in a language. For example, I understood from Cummins (1984) that, for my students, a face-to-face conversation about the price of peaches with the produce man at the local supermarket is a relatively easy task because it's imbued with visual and paralinguistic cues—because, in Cummins's words, it is so "context embedded." (I should have understood this from my experience with French in Tunisia, but, strangely, I didn't make the connection.)

Along the same continuum, I could see that a school task requiring students to read a bare text (unaccompanied by pictures, charts, or diagrams)—that is, a text wholly dependent on linguistic cues for its understanding—is difficult for anyone but the most proficient readers, because it is so greatly "context reduced." As a result, I began to make sure that beginning-level student readers could "see" the semantic flow of a text (through pictures) before relying on printed words. And I renewed my efforts to build in class time for student writers to orally "rehearse" ideas for writing in peer-pair work before confronting bare sheets of paper.

From Cummins, I also learned that students' "know-how" in meeting increasingly complex reading/writing school demands, if developed in their first language, can then *transfer* to the second language. But that this academic know-how develops *only* in text-rich and content-rich environments. I could then see that some (often "international" students) come into our ESL composition classes with this academic literacy already developed in L1 and some (often USA-educated ESL students) do not.

Finally, from Cummins, I began to understand how it is that the conversational fluency of some ESL (again, immigrant) students masks their lack of academic literacy to the point where they were prematurely mainstreamed—and no longer provided the ESL instruction they still needed—long before leaving local high schools. And that the challenge for college ESL writing programs is to help them gain the reading/writing know-how they need to cope with college course demands, and without which they will surely fail. (See Blanton and Lee, 1998, for an attempt to shape instructional materials to meet these needs.)

Living an ESL life in the 1980s meant struggling through such newfound awareness of language and literacy issues, as theory and teaching suddenly became much more complex. Cognitivist researchers like Krashen and Cummins were shaking us up. Not coincidentally, at about the same time, immigrant ESL students poured into college-level ESL writing classes. (See Harklau, Losey, & Siegal, 1999, for a discussion of these students, lately referred to as "Generation 1.5.") I hardly think we knew what hit us—either in terms of cognitive theory or (more so, in the trenches) immigrant ESL students.

The upshot was that, even if ESL composition teachers still proceeded to teach as if all students were international students with academically literate backgrounds, we *were* becoming aware that international students were no longer the only ESL learners on the planet. (Practice was disconnected from reality.) It also began to dawn on us that, even for international students, we could no longer blindly assume that if we only helped them *speak* English and corrected their grammar on paper, everything else would then take care of itself. Our understanding of the actual literacy needs of immigrant students would take longer to emerge, by at least another decade.

About 1980s ESL in general, let me say that it was first in the work related to bilingual *children* that cognitive theory had its greatest impact. Researchers like Anna Uhl Chamot (1987), Lily Wong-Fillmore (1979), Shirley Brice Heath (1980, 1982), and Virginia Collier (1987)—all working within a cognitive framework—addressed the needs of immigrant children, particularly their literacy needs, and contributed to the field's greater understanding. *(Thought I had forgotten about you, Dr. B.? Maybe I did get a bit carried away with cognitive theory. But I see you're pleased about the children. I'm not surprised. I know you wrote reading materials for kids . . . How do I know? The son of an old friend of yours told me.)*

Looking for a Home for Second Language Writing

Earlier I said that a shift in perspective from teaching to learning in the 1980s rearranged the landscape of ESL instruction. That students' academic needs, cognitive development, purposes for language use, literacy growth, and stress levels and feelings (as impacting their learning) all began to matter. This is true, but not completely.

It *is* true for those at the forefront of developing pedagogies and materials for second language children. And it *is* true for those at the forefront of developing curriculum for adults with specialized language needs, that is, in ESP. It is *not* necessarily true for second language writing instruction at the college level, that is, for ESL composition. Given its historical exclusion from applied linguistics, L2 composition did not develop in sync with ESL. (See Paul Kei Matsuda, 1998, 1999, for a thorough discussion.) This is not surprising, but it is no less complicating.

In truth, ESL composition, like a foster child, has been hard to "place." Not present at the birth of ESL, in fact, not a natural-born child of linguistics, it has been shunted between foster homes in English departments, ELIs, skill centers, and extension programs (taught alongside belly dancing and wine tasting). Does ESL composition belong in an intensive ESL program? Should it be part of an English department's freshman composition offering? Should it be part of a school's remedial writing program (read: "service burden")? Nobody seems to know.

These unresolved questions bring us to the present. While waiting for Godot, college program administrators have created jerry-rigged curricular constructs that perch second language students precariously between institutional units, both in and out of the academic mainstream. At the sister institution to mine, international students do not academically matriculate into the university until they exit intensive ESL, which is attached to the university in satellite fashion, as nonacademic, noncredit. However, state-resident ESL students who do not place immediately in "regular" freshman writing classes *are* academically admitted to the university, if they otherwise qualify, and *they* take noncredit English department writing courses designed to prepare them for freshman English.

This convoluted arrangement is similar to that at my own institution—with some ESL courses inside English, others outside the department. As a result, professional toes are stepped on all the time, no matter how gracefully the dancers pirouette. ESL students—whether international or resident—don't understand how the system works or how and why they end up placed where they do. No wonder. (*Still with me, Dr. B.? Pardon my irreverence.*)

Also in the meantime—several decades of meantime—ESL writing/reading, disconnected as it was from "regular" ESL, attached itself (as it grew) to first language writing, that is, to the field of rhetoric/composition. In this collection, Ilona Leki and Ann M. Johns tell their stories of marriage to the modes and then to process writing. Like surviving divorcees, they relate their transitions through stages of regret but good riddance, to relief, and now to wonderment about the future. Their experience is not unique. It is the experience of most of us in second language writing. It is also largely the trajectory of (L1) composition studies, which L2 writing has shadowed.

I too have been there, done that, but bent as I am on taking the long view, I will bypass close-up details of my own transitions in classroom teaching. Let me say generally that ESL composition teachers, realizing the need to profit from L1 composition studies yet forge a new path, have spent the past two decades (at least) searching and experimenting. Seeing how, in fact, the needs of second language writers may differ from those of first language writers, a difference Tony Silva (1993, 1997) has written a good deal about.

Coming of Age

I mark the debut of L2 writing's higher visibility in ESL as the early 1990s—particularly with the publication of Barbara Kroll's *Second Language Writing* (1990)—but, in fact, Barbara and others were busy before then. TESOL's 1995 annotated bibliography of publications on L2 writing lists four-hun-dred-and-sev-en-ty-eight *pages* of references (Tannacito, 1995). (*I'm saying it slowly for effect, Dr. B.*) Although the bulk of the citations *are* from the 1990s, some date back to the 1970s. (For example, Ann Raimes, 1978, and Vivian Zamel, 1976, known— along with Barbara Kroll, 1978—for their work in ESL writing, began publishing on the topic in the 1970s.) Yet, it seems we've only *begun* to understand the difficulties of preparing college-level L2 writers for academic success.

Our new questions are many and even more complex. I voice but a few. Increasingly aware of the gulf between writing instruction and real-world language uses and needs (despite much good work in ESP), we ask what those needs are. Better yet, we ask how we can prepare students for success in our *own* academic institutions. If an ESL program's goals are academic reading and writing, how then do we teach the intellectual operations (Cummins's academic literacy)—teach the thinking processes nurtured by and reflected in written language—that are expected of successful college students? What *is* critical/academic literacy anyway? And can it even be taught? And, lastly, how in the world do we accommodate the needs of immigrant USA-educated ESL students who enter community colleges and open-admission universities without well-developed literacy in *any* language, either English or the home language, a question I have struggled to address (Blanton, 1992, 1994, 1999, 2001b)?

And now, as the paradigm shifts again—as we look at individuals no longer in isolation but in relation to communities—we ask what it means to consider writing as social practice, as shaped by the cultural communities in which it takes place. (It's too early to know the impact on classrooms.) As we talk about the "situated-ness" of writing (that is, writing within its social and cultural context), we are seeing the cognitive model, while still valid, as limited, and autonomous writers as a fiction. Instead, as we begin to put it, academic and work-related writing engages whole persons "at the intersection of language, cognition, *and* culture." (The twentieth century carried us well into language and cognition. The twenty-first finds us wading into culture concerns or, depending on whom you ask, already swimming in their midst.)

Earlier (in a broad sense), structural linguistics' application, codified as audio-lingual methodology, was overtaken by behaviorist psychology. Behaviorism subsequently came up against cognitive psychology (and transformational linguistics) and was overtaken. Now, cognitive psychology meets social theory. Not quite parallel, but Leonard Bloomfield to

Noam Chomsky, Chomsky to the Brazilian social activist–educator Paulo Freire (1970) and the Russian social-cognitive psychologist Lev Vygotsky (1977). (*We'll need to talk again, Dr. B. I'm leaving out a lot, I know. And, lest I mislead you, Vygotsky wasn't your junior. My little timeline doesn't really work. But, you see, Vygotsky's work didn't reach the West until much later. And, by the way, I'm sorry your work got mixed up with B. F. Skinner's.*)

Beyond Methodology

So where *is* ESL? At a crossroads, as I see it. Actually, we're already headed down the path envisioned in 1996, when the conversation among the narrators of this collection first began. Given our accumulated knowledge and experience, we ESL writing teachers had already reached (by the mid-1990s) the limits of our several-decades-old conception of ourselves. In fact, our conception had begun to delimit us.

By mentally positioning ourselves almost exclusively within the confines of the classroom, we focused too narrowly: How to teach writing? How to respond to writing? How to build in the writing process? How to incorporate readings into writing? Whether or not to peer edit? Don't get me wrong—these are important questions—but *how-to* and *whether-or-not* are not everything. The ESL domain need not be circumscribed by methodology, by what we do in the classroom.

The legacy of beginning as an applied field, with those in the "parent" field of linguistics doing the research and creating theory, became a ball and chain. (*Sorry to be blunt, Dr. B., but actually it wasn't your doing. It just worked out that way.*) Linguists concern(ed) themselves with, among other things, the nature and structure and varieties of language, not with language instruction. And ESL, separated as it was at birth from theory making, operated in a vacuum, focusing on pedagogy yet disconnected from broader intellectual understanding. We didn't know at first how to make theory for ourselves or that theory making was possible, even necessary. (And with ESL writing unclear in its relationship to ESL, can the situation get any more complex?)

Mind you, linguistics is a valuable field, but, I must say, the initial relationship between linguistics and ESL was a mixed blessing. (*Sorry again.*) The positive is, rather obviously, that greater ESL evolved from a field devoted to language, as compared, say, to "foreign" language instruction, which developed as a satellite of literature. Enough said about that.

About the negatives, let me say more. In concerning ourselves almost exclusively with figuring out how to teach writing (or reading, or anything, but in this essay I'm most concerned with writing) and teach it effectively, we paid an intellectual price. For one, we were slow to understand writing in terms of literacy. To see reading and writing as indivisible. To understand that reading and writing don't develop from discrete pieces of language. To grasp that reading and writing are social-cognitive acts, not wholly realizable through textbook exercises or preconceptualized topics and content. That some students enter our ESL classroom having already created literate worlds for themselves, but many have not. And that our challenge as reading-writing teachers lies in more fully understanding the role of literacy in people's lives, our own included, and translating that into creating domains for literate learning for our students.

For another, we were slow—are still being slow—to build a discipline, a field, but the pace is picking up. While we have talked a lot about a discipline, our discussions have been more about *practice*. I think the mistake has been in mis-taking practice—*how to*—for the discipline itself. (And by "the discipline," I mean the whole of applied linguistics, of which I see ESL/EFL, including second language writing, to be a primary part.)

Advancing the Discipline

As we develop a discipline, we are, at the same time, learning from each other's experiences and reflections. This is not coincidental: one is a condition for the other. (As I write, I am overwhelmed by trying to gain a perspective on our current selves while looking from inside the bubble of everyday academic life. But let me try.) Although I may say later that, yes, that *was* silly, I'll venture four suggestions for keeping the momentum of discipline building going.

- Let's not just talk practice—that is, exchange information on *how to*—let's also talk *about* practice. This means reflecting on what we do, on the results we get or don't get, on what we know from each other. Reflect on the kind of learning we want our students to experience. And reflect on what students themselves say about that experience. Talking about practice requires us to let down our guard and stop fretting about whether we're doing it right. Whether someone will come along and say we're doing it wrong. Everyone has something to contribute.
- Let's not only report on research. Let's also write reflective pieces and exploratory essays in which we wrestle with our experiences, perceptions, and concerns. We are beginning to do this. (Take, for instance, this collection.) We need to continue wondering aloud about what we know, what we're doing, and what we want to do. And write about what our students think about their learning and where and how it fits into their education and, indeed, into their lives. In the academy and in our profession, we need to treat research reporting and reflection as equally valuable. Lest we con-

tinue to lose valuable insights and effective means for critiquing ourselves, let's toss out the attitude that reflective writing is mere personal writing and, therefore, not objective or dispassionate enough to be "academic." Otherwise, we risk silencing those whose voices help build a rich, inclusive, and thoughtful professional discipline.

- Let's value qualitative research, as we have quantitative research. We are beginning to do this. Let's think harder about treating both as "scholarly." We need to toss out the untenable separation between theory and practice institutionalized in professional journals and in our thinking. Practice and theory are inextricably bound: out of theory grows practice; out of practice, theory. Stories, descriptions, conversations, interviews, ethnographies, and case studies all contribute to theoretical insight and understanding, as surely as quantitative studies.
- Let's connect classrooms to communities, where we all live our lives. Experience is a powerful teacher. Creating language and literacy lessons through community research and activities can do more for ESL learners than almost anything we provide within the confines of the classroom. The barrier between classroom and community is artificial, but we've treated it as impermeable. Tear it down. For example, Shirley Brice Heath, at Stanford, has freshman students working in and writing about battered women's shelters. Edith Babin, at Louisiana State University, the sister institution of my own, has ESL students writing stories for children in a daycare center, stories they tell the children and the children tell them. Then Edith's students critique, in writing, the success of their work with the kids. Others are doing equally interesting work, but, my point is, there is just not enough yet.

I leave you with the following. Surely a discipline is, in large part, a history, with both present and past dimensions.

And creating a history involves storytelling, as indicated in the French word *histoire,* from which *story* derives. So we build a discipline by constructing a history, and we construct a history, in part, by telling stories about language and literacy experiences. About our students. About ourselves.

> *That is my tale, Dr. Bloomfield. You had no idea? Well, a lot has gone on. . . . Your legacy? Above all, I'd say, our sense of the systematic nature of language. Understanding dialects as language variation. Viewing language as patterned behavior. You saw language in its cultural context, you know. . . . By the way, I met your sisters-in-law late in their lives. Had dinner at their house. I could barely eat, I was so awed. Your picture was hanging in the dining room. They spoke very fondly of you. I thought you'd like to know.*

References

Asher, J. (1982). *Learning another language through actions: The complete teacher's guidebook.* (2nd ed.). Los Gatos, CA: Sky Oaks Productions.

Blanton, L. L. (1977). *Beginning composition practice.* Books 1–2. Rowley, MA: Newbury House.

Blanton, L. L. (1978). *Intermediate composition practice.* Books 1–2. Rowley, MA: Newbury House.

Blanton, L. L. (1988). *Idea exchange.* Books 1–2. Boston: Harper & Row.

Blanton, L. L. (1992). Reading, writing, and authority: Issues in developmental ESL. *College ESL, 2 (1),* 11–19.

Blanton, L. L. (1994). Discourse, artifacts, and the Ozarks: Understanding academic literacy. *Journal of Second Language Writing, 3,* 1–16.

Blanton, L. L. (1999). Classroom instruction and language minority students: Teaching to "smarter" readers and writers. In L. Harklau, K. M. Losey, & M. Siegal (Eds.), *Generation 1.5 meets college composition* (pp. 119–142). Mahwah, NJ: Lawrence Erlbaum Associates.

Blanton, L. L. (2001a). *Composition practice.* Books 1–4 (3rd ed.). Boston: Heinle & Heinle.

Blanton, L. L. (2001b). *Idea exchange.* Books 1–2 (2nd ed.). Boston: Heinle & Heinle.

Blanton, L. L., & Lee, L. (1998). *Writing workshop: Promoting college success.* Boston: Heinle & Heinle.

Bloomfield, L. (1914/1983). *An introduction to the study of language* (2nd ed.). Amsterdam, Philadelphia: John Benjamins.

Bloomfield, L. (1933). *Language.* New York: Henry Holt.

Chamot, A. U. (1987). The cognitive academic language learning approach: A bridge to the mainstream. *TESOL Quarterly, 21,* 227–249.

Chomsky, N. (1957). *Syntactic structures.* The Hague: Mouton.

Chomsky, N. (1966). *Cartesian linguistics: A chapter in the history of rationalist thought.* Lanham, MD: University Press of America.

Coffey, M. P. (1983). *Fitting in: A functional/notional text for learners of English.* Englewood Cliffs, NJ: Prentice-Hall.

Collier, V. (1987). Age and rate of acquisition of second language for academic purposes. *TESOL Quarterly, 21,* 617–641.

Costinett, S. (1970). *Structure graded readings in English.* Books 1–2. N.p.: Gemini Books.

Cummins, J. (1976). The influence of bilingualism on cognitive growth: A synthesis of research findings and explanatory hypotheses. *Working Papers on Bilingualism, 9,* 1–43.

Cummins, J. (1979). Cognitive/academic language proficiency, linguistic interdependence, the optimum age question and some other matters. *Working Papers on Bilingualism, 19,* 121–129.

Cummins, J. (1984). *Bilingualism and special education: Issues in assessment and pedagogy.* San Diego: College Hill.

Franklin, H. B., Meikle, H. G., & Strain, J. E. (1967). *Vocabulary in context.* Ann Arbor: University of Michigan Press.

Freire, P. (1970). *Pedagogy of the oppressed.* New York: Continuum.

Fries, C. C. (1945). *Teaching and learning English as a foreign language.* Ann Arbor: University of Michigan Press.

Harklau, L., Losey, K. M. & Siegal, M. (Eds.). (1999). *Generation 1.5 meets college composition.* Mahwah, NJ: Lawrence Erlbaum Associates.

Heath, S. B. (1980). The functions and uses of literacy. *Journal of Communication, 30,* 123–133.

Heath, S. B. (1982). Ethnography in education: Defining the essentials. In P. Gilmore & A. A. Glatthorn, (Eds.), *Children in and out of school: Ethnography and education* (pp. 33–55). Washington, DC: Center for Applied Linguistics.

Krashen, S. (1978). The monitor model for second-language acquisition. In R. C. Gingras (Ed.), *Second-language acquisition and foreign language teaching* (pp. 1–26). Arlington, VA: Center for Applied Linguistics.

Krashen, S. (1982). *Principles and practice in second language acquisition.* Elmsford, NY: Pergamon Press.

Krashen, S. (1984). *Writing, research, theory, and applications.* Oxford: Pergamon.

Krashen, S., & Terrell, T. (1983). *The natural approach: Language acquisition in the classroom.* Hayward, CA: Alemany Press.

Krohn, R. (1972). *English sentence structure.* Ann Arbor: University of Michigan Press.

Kroll, B. (1978). Sorting out writing problems. In C. Blatchford & J. Schachter (Eds.), *On TESOL '78: EFL policies, programs, practices* (pp. 176–182). Washington, DC: TESOL.

Kroll, B. (1979). Learning and acquisition: Two paths to writing. *English Education, 11,* 83–90.

Kroll, B. (Ed.). (1990). *Second language writing: Research insights for the classroom.* New York: Cambridge University Press.

Lado, R., & Fries, C. C. (1943). *English pattern practices.* Ann Arbor: University of Michigan Press.

Lado, R., & Fries, C. C. (1954). *English pronunciation.* Ann Arbor: University of Michigan Press.

Lado, R., & Fries, C. C. (1958). *English pattern practice.* Ann Arbor: University of Michigan Press.

Lawrence, M. S. (1972). *Writing as a thinking process.* Ann Arbor: University of Michigan Press.

Lyons, J. (1970). *Noam Chomsky.* New York: Viking Press.

Matsuda, P. K. (1998). Situating ESL writing in a cross-disciplinary context. *Written Communication, 15,* 99–121.

Matsuda, P. K. (1999). Composition studies and ESL writing: A disciplinary division of labor. *College Composition and Communication, 50,* 699–721.

Paulston, C. B., & Bruder, M. N. (1975). *From substitution to substance: A handbook of structural pattern drills.* Rowley, MA: Newbury House.

Raimes, A. (1978). *Problems and strategies in ESL composition (If Johnny has problems, what about Juan, Jean and Ywe-Han?)* Language in Education, Theory and Practice, No. 14. Englewood Cliffs, NJ: Prentice Hall.

Raimes, A. (1987). *Exploring through writing.* New York: St. Martin's Press.

Silva, T. (1993). Toward an understanding of the distinct nature of second language writing: The ESL research and its implications. *TESOL Quarterly, 27,* 657–677. Reprinted in T. Silva & P. K. Matsuda (Eds.). (2001). *Landmark essays on ESL writing.* Mahwah, NJ: Lawrence Erlbaum Associates.

Silva, T. (1997). Differences in ESL and native-English-speaker writing: The research and its implications. In C. Severino, J. C. Guerra, & J. E. Butler (Eds.), *Writing in multicultural settings* (pp. 209–219). New York: MLA.

Swales, J. (1971). *Writing scientific English.* Ontario, Canada: Nelson.

Tannacito, D. J. (1995). *A guide to writing English as a second or foreign language: An annotated bibliography of research and pedagogy.* Alexandria, VA: TESOL.

Trimble, M. T., Trimble, L., & Drobnic, K. (Eds.). (1978). *English for specific purposes: Science and technology.* Corvallis, OR: English Language Institute, Oregon State University.

Vygotsky, L. (1977). *Thought and language* (2nd ed.). Cambridge, MA: MIT Press.

Wong-Fillmore, L. (1979). Individual differences in second language acquisition. In C. J. Fillmore, D. Kempler, & W. S-Y. Wang (Eds.), *Individual differences in language ability and language behavior* (pp. 203–228). New York: Academic Press.

Zamel, V. (1976). Teaching composition in the ESL classroom: What we can learn from research in the teaching of English. *TESOL Quarterly, 10,* 67–76.

Paul Kei Matsuda always wanted to become a teacher. In elementary school, he wanted to become an elementary school teacher and, in junior high school, a junior high school teacher. At the age of 17, when he realized that the best learning strategy was to teach himself, he became his own first student, teaching himself English primarily through reading and writing. He has been teaching ever since, while continuing to teach himself how to teach.

Epilogue
Reinventing Giants

Paul Kei Matsuda
University of New Hampshire

We are like dwarfs perched on the shoulders of giants; thus we are able to see more and farther than they can, not because we have keener eyesight, or stand taller, but because we are raised and lifted aloft on their gigantic greatness.—Bernard of Chartres

These Are the Stories of Giants in the Making

The *teaching* of writing to non-native speakers of English had already become a serious concern at some institutions of U.S. higher education by the early 1960s (Matsuda, 1999, 2001), but the *field* of second language writing took longer to develop. That is, even though, from the 1960s on, second language writing courses were being taught (particularly in ESL contexts), textbooks were being written, and teachers and researchers were making conference presentations on topics related to the field, the idea of second language writing as a field with its own disciplinary infrastructure and a shared sense of identity did not come into prominence until the

1990s. The birth of the field, at least in my mind, is marked most conspicuously by the publication of Barbara Kroll's landmark collection, *Second Language Writing: Research Insights for the Classroom* (1990) and the creation, in 1992, of the *Journal of Second Language Writing,* edited by Ilona Leki and Tony Silva. Prominent in these and other important publications in the field are the names of many of the giants represented in the present collection.

Giants they are indeed. The authors whose tales are told in this volume have had many years of experience as teachers of ESL writing. Some, in fact, have been teaching for as long as I have lived, if not longer. As I was developing my own expertise as a teacher and scholar of second language writing, I read and learned from many of their works, hoping to build on their collective wisdom in my own work. As teacher educators, they have nurtured generations of ESL writing teachers, some of whom have gone on to become teacher educators themselves. Many of them have also mentored budding scholars who themselves are now seeking to contribute to the growing body of knowledge in the field. I, too, received my professional preparation under the superb guidance of one whose tale appears in this book. I have also gained much from the informal and often indirect mentorship of others represented here.

As these stories attest, however, their narrators have not always been the giants they are today. Believe it or not, they were once young and inexperienced teachers; and many of them became teachers of ESL writing quite by accident. They, too, struggled with issues of authority, or the lack thereof, in the classroom. When they walked into the ESL writing classroom for the first time, they probably were as nervous as any brand-new teacher. A number of them started teaching ESL writing when few ESL writing textbooks were available. And when handed a textbook to use, some of them tried, as many novice teachers would, to teach the textbook faithfully, only to realize later that teaching "by the book" does not always yield the desired outcome because contexts of instruction often vary beyond what textbooks are designed to accommodate. Furthermore, they realized that early textbooks were not necessarily informed by adequate theories of writing. Faced with a lack of workable alternatives, some of the giants developed their own textbooks, many of which are still being widely used today.

In the absence of well-developed theories of writing in TESL/TEFL, a number of them turned to first language composition studies and even received formal professional preparation in composition theories and pedagogies; however, they also came to realize that pedagogies and materials developed with only monolingual native-English-speaking (NES) writers in mind do not always work for second language writers, who come from diverse linguistic and cultural backgrounds and whose learning goals are not necessarily the same as those of their NES peers. When they figured out that neither composition studies nor TESL alone could provide the kinds of insight necessary to inform their work, they began to create their own discourse community. Thus, the field of second language writing was born.

All of the giants whose voices we hear in this volume have traveled far in search of better pedagogies and, in time, better theories. Some of them sought the shoulders of their own giants to perch on, such as those of Robert Kaplan or Clifford Prator. They followed fads and fashions in pedagogical approaches and strategies, adopted new innovations with enthusiasm, were disillusioned by their limitations, and then moved on to other, "new and improved" pedagogies. As Dana Ferris notes in the introduction to this collection, Tony Silva aptly characterizes this development as the "merry-go-round of approaches" that generated "more heat than light" (Silva, 1990, p. 18). Eventually, they came to recognize the complexity of second language writing and writing instruction and began to develop a more critical and reflective attitude toward their own teaching practices. They also realized the need to develop more theoretically grounded approaches and materials and sought to better understand the nature of second language writing, writers, and writing instruction by engaging in research efforts and theoretical discussions.

Thanks to the hard work of these giants (and others), we now have a wide array of professional resources to draw on. We have numerous textbooks to choose from, representing various pedagogical approaches and covering a wide range of proficiency levels and student needs. Opportunities for professional preparation in the teaching of second language writing have expanded considerably during the last decade or so, with an increasing number of master's programs now offering courses in the teaching of second language writing. And we also have doctoral programs where graduate students can work under the guidance of some of the second language writing specialists represented in this volume, including Alister Cumming at Ontario Institute for Studies in Education/University of Toronto, Tony Silva at Purdue University, and myself at the University of New Hampshire. Finally, we have professional books for second language writing teachers and researchers widely available, and books of this sort continue to proliferate (e.g., Carson & Leki, 1993; Ferris & Hedgcock, 1998; Kroll, 1990; Leki, 1992; Reid, 1993; Silva, Brice, & Reichelt, 1999; Silva & Matsuda, 2001a, 2001b, and see the Michigan Series on Teaching Multilingual Writers, series editors Diane Belcher and Jun Liu). We, the newer generations of second language writing teachers and scholars, now stand firmly on the shoulders of giants—or so it may seem.

This Is Not, However, the Story of Dwarfs Perched on Their Shoulders

When I was asked to write this epilogue, my initial impulse was to use the metaphor of dwarfs ("we") perched on the shoulders of giants ("them"). After all, they are the people who created the field in which I work. Yet, while there is no question about their being giants, the image of dwarfs standing on their shoulders doesn't work too well. It is not just because, at least physically, I, for one, stand taller and probably have better eyesight than they. Rather, it has to do with the particular way newcomers continue to enter the profession, as well as the way all teachers develop knowledge.

While second language writing has come to be recognized by many as a field of specialization, especially at the college level, it has not been—and perhaps it will never be—institutionalized as a popular career path in the way that some people may think of a future in teaching in general. It is almost inconceivable that children would dream of becoming ESL *writing* teachers the way they dream of becoming perhaps some other kind of teacher. While some future ESL writing teachers may be introduced to the field by working in writing centers that serve a diverse population or even by taking ESL writing courses themselves, they are probably not the norm. Many still "stumble" into ESL writing, just as many of the giants did.

In fact, new teachers continue to find themselves teaching ESL writing unexpectedly, struggling with issues similar to those faced by the giants. I am no exception. I began my "career" as an ESL writing teacher also by happenstance during my first year of undergraduate studies in Wisconsin. As a favor to some friends who were also ESL writers, I provided tutoring services, going over their papers, pointing out grammar errors and various other "problems." I sometimes gave them minilectures on grammar, usage, thesis statements, topic sentences, organization, and other topics that interested me at any given moment. I also spent several summers tutoring English to high-school and college students in Japan. As I developed my pedagogy, I drew on my own experience as an ESL writer, as well as on examples set by my teachers—both ESL teachers and non-ESL writing teachers. It was not until some years later (in my senior year in college) that I received some formal preparation as a writing tutor at the university writing center.

As a writing tutor who lacked a broad understanding of various theoretical perspectives in the field, I was susceptible to the kinds of pendulum swings that some of these giants describe. There were times when I focused almost exclusively on the issues of grammar and style; then there were times when I went to the other extreme, refusing to comment on grammar issues at all. After taking a business writing class, I started emphasizing the use of short sentences and active voice, condemning the kind of academic prose that I now read and write daily (with a great sense of pleasure and excitement, I might add). There also was a time when I was excited about identifying linguistic and cultural rhetorical patterns in the texts of my tutees. At one point, I was so disgusted by the overemphasis on grammar in some ESL writing classrooms that I was opposed to teaching English "as a second language" altogether. However, as I gained more experience tutoring both native and non-native English speakers at the writing center, I began to realize that strategies developed to help native English speakers—such as asking questions or having students read their own texts aloud to identify grammar errors—didn't always work well with second language writers.

As was the case with many of the giants, I started reading the professional literature on second language writing on my own. (At this point, I was working toward my master's degree in composition and rhetoric at Miami University of Ohio; see Matsuda, in press.) Reading the literature on second language writing was necessary for me because, to do a good job as a writing tutor, I felt the need to understand more about second language writers and writing instruction, even though I was not being introduced to such literature in my master's program. (It was concerned primarily with NES writers.) Ultimately, as a result of my self-directed study—and especially after taking a graduate seminar in second language writing taught by Tony Silva during the first year of my doctoral studies at Purdue—I felt fairly well versed and prepared by the time I started teaching ESL writing in a classroom setting. I had all the theoretical and pedagogical resources I needed at my disposal; in addition, I had the benefit of being mentored by one of the giants.

Having professional preparation, resources, and mentoring were certainly helpful. For instance, I did know—both from my own experience as an ESL student and from working with Tony—not to "teach the textbook" but rather to use textbooks as resources. I also knew that it wasn't the end of the world when my written feedback to students was not reflected in their second drafts or when students didn't seem to be using peer workshops productively. Yet, for the most part, I credit my years of experience as an ESL writing tutor and ESL writer myself as having laid the groundwork that allowed me to gain as much from the professional preparation as I did.

I don't mean to suggest that I didn't benefit from the professional preparation I received. I do believe, as Barbara Kroll suggests in her tale, that new generations of second language writing teachers should take advantage of available professional preparation opportunities and resources in order to guide and even accelerate their development as teachers. However, no amount of professional preparation or resources will help new teachers see farther than the giants can see today unless new teachers themselves are willing to struggle with various issues and develop their own personal knowledge base, situated as it is in the context of their own teaching.

And walk in our own shoes we must. Even when we trace the paths created by these giants—seeing the same scenery they saw and making some of the same wrong turns they made—we will have to discover for ourselves what we know and where we are going. We will eventually reach some of the same conclusions: that teaching is a complex business, that we need to be critical and reflective, that we will continue to face the same challenges that we faced when we began, and that we nevertheless have to continue to walk forward as these giants so clearly have done. And we will see that we have to create this knowledge for ourselves. It cannot simply be handed down to us. When we come to these realizations, we will have reinvented ourselves as giants. And we will see farther and know more because we are seeing through the eyes of giants, not from their shoulders. The nature of *becoming* is that, in part, we also must start from scratch, although we have the tales of the giants to guide us in the process.

We must all become giants ourselves. Each of us.

References

Carson, J. G., & Leki, I. (Eds.). (1993). *Reading in the composition classroom: Second language perspective*. Boston: Heinle & Heinle.

Ferris, D., & Hedgcock, J. (1998). *Teaching ESL composition*. Mahwah, NJ: Laurence Erlbaum Associates.

Kroll, B. (Ed.). (1990). *Second language writing: Research insights for the classroom*. New York: Cambridge University Press.

Leki, I. (1992). *Understanding ESL writers: A guide for teachers*. Portsmouth, NH: Boynton/Cook Heinemann.

Leki, I., & Silva, T. (Eds.). (1992). *Journal of Second Language Writing*. New York: Elsevier Science.

Matsuda, P. K. (1999). Composition studies and ESL writing: A disciplinary division of labor. *College Composition and Communication, 50*, 699–721.

Matsuda, P. K. (2001). Reexamining audiolingualism: On the genesis of reading and writing in L2 studies. In D. Belcher & A. Hirvela (Eds.), *Linking literacies: Perspectives on L2 reading-writing connections* (pp. 84–105). Ann Arbor: University of Michigan Press.

Matsuda, P. K. (In press). Coming to voice: Writing as a graduate student. In C. P. Casanave & S. Vandrick (Eds.). *Writing for scholarly publication: Behind the scenes in language education*. Mahwah, NJ: Lawrence Erlbaum Associates.

Reid, J. M. (1993). *Teaching ESL writing.* Englewood Cliffs, NJ: Regents/Prentice Hall.

Silva, T. (1990). Second language composition instruction: Developments, issues, and directions in ESL. In B. Kroll (Ed.), *Second language writing: Research insights for the classroom* (pp. 11–23). New York: Cambridge University Press.

Silva, T., Brice, C., & Reichelt, M. (Eds.). (1999). *Annotated bibliography of scholarship in second language writing: 1993–1997.* Stamford, CT: Ablex.

Silva, T., & Matsuda, P. K. (Eds.). (2001a). *Landmark essays on ESL writing.* Mahwah, NJ: Lawrence Erlbaum Associates.

Silva, T., & Matsuda, P. K. (Eds.). (2001b). *On second language writing.* Mahwah, NJ: Lawrence Erlbaum Associates.

Contributors

Linda Lonon Blanton is professor of English and director of the University Honors Program at the University of New Orleans. With a research interest in second language literacy and composition, her current focus is Generation 1.5/ESL writers. She has authored or coauthored three series of ESL composition textbooks, of which *Composition Practice* (Heinle & Heinle, 2001, 3rd ed.) has been in the field the longest. She is also the author of *Varied Voices: On Language and Literacy Learning* (Heinle & Heinle, 1998), an ethnographic study of multilingual children in Morocco, and articles in *College ESL* and the *Journal of Second Language Writing.*

Alister Cumming is professor and head of the Modern Language Centre at the Ontario Institute for Studies in Education of the University of Toronto. He teaches graduate courses and conducts research on second language writing, student assessment, and curriculum evaluation, particularly for English as a second/foreign language.

Melinda Erickson is a lecturer in the division of College Writing Programs at the University of California, Berkeley. Her teaching includes courses in reading and composition for first and second language undergraduates, grammar and vocabulary for second language writers, composition pedagogy for graduates, and TEFL methodology for international teachers. She is a fellow of the Bay Area Writing Project, a consultant for the Educational Testing Service, and a frequent conference presenter on particular areas of interest: composition, assessment, articulation, and undiagnosed learning disabilities among second language writers.

Dana Ferris is professor of English at California State University, Sacramento, where she teaches courses in ESL and linguistics and directs the ESL composition program. She is coauthor with John Hedgcock of *Teaching ESL Composition* (Erlbaum, 1998) and author of two new books, *Treatment of Error in Second Language Writing Classes* (University of Michigan Press, 2002) and *Response to Student Writing* (Erlbaum, 2002).

Ann M. Johns is professor of linguistics and writing studies, and director of the Center for Teaching and Learning at San Diego State University. She has been publishing articles and books on the teaching and learning of L2 writing for many years. Her most recent are *Text, Role, and Context: Developing Academic Literacies* (Cambridge, 1997) and an edited volume, *Genre in the Classroom: Multiple Perspectives* (Erlbaum, 2002).

Barbara Kroll is professor of English and linguistics at California State University, Northridge. Her teaching and research interests focus on training new teachers of college composition to both native and non-native speakers of English. In addition to publishing in the areas of ESL/EFL writing, she has made frequent presentations at annual TESOL conventions and the

Conference on College Composition and Communication (CCCC), dating back to 1978. She serves on the editorial boards for the journals *Assessing Writing* and the *Journal of Second Language Writing.* And she recently edited *Exploring the Dynamics of Second Language Writing* (Cambridge University Press, 2003), a collection of scholarly papers providing a basic introduction to the field.

Ilona Leki teaches and does research at the University of Tennessee. She has taught and learned from students and teachers in the United States, France, Morocco, Colombia, Turkey, Yugoslavia, Brazil, Hong Kong, and Egypt. Her research centers on trying to understand what the process of developing academic literacy in a second language entails and to use that understanding to help make academic writing in English a comfortable and rewarding experience for second language students and fruitful reading for their teachers.

Paul Kei Matsuda is assistant professor of English at the University of New Hampshire, where he teaches undergraduate writing courses and graduate courses in composition studies and applied linguistics. With Tony Silva, he founded and chairs the Symposium on Second Language Writing and edited *Landmark Essays on ESL Writing* (Erlbaum, 2001) and *On Second Language Writing* (Erlbaum, 2001). Paul has published in journals such as *College Composition and Communication,* the *Journal of Second Language Writing,* and *Written Communication.*

Joy Reid is professor of English at the University of Wyoming, where she directs the ESL support program and teaches ESL methods, linguistics, and writing. She has published an ESL composition textbook series and a reference book, *Teaching ESL Writing* (Prentice Hall, 1993) and she has edited two anthologies about learning styles and coauthored with Pat Byrd the book *Grammar in the Composition Classroom* (Heinle, 1998). Her other research interests include discourse analysis, the change process, and the differences between international and U.S.-resident ESL students. Currently she is coediting an ESL series for residents, with Pat Byrd and Cynthia Schuemann.

Tony Silva is associate professor of ESL in the Department of English at Purdue University, where he directs the ESL writing program and teaches undergraduate and graduate courses for ESL students and ESL teachers. With Ilona Leki, he founded and edits the *Journal of Second Language Writing.* With Paul Kei Matsuda, he founded and hosts the Symposium on Second Language Writing and edited *Landmark Essays in ESL Writing* (Erlbaum, 2001) and *On Second Language Writing* (Erlbaum, 2001). And with Colleen Brice and Melinda Reichelt, he compiled the *Annotated Bibliography of Scholarship on Second Language Writing* (Ablex, 1999).

Index

target language community, 127, 128
task-based writing instruction, 74, 77, 90, 127
teachers
  as advocates, 59–61
  and balance, 10
  critical thinking and, 58, 98
  professional development of, 134
  self-reflection by, 39, 44, 45, 47, 56, 60–61, 81, 100–101, 157–158, 165, 170
  training of (see training of teachers)
Teachers of English to Speakers of Other Languages (TESOL), 1, 18, 35n, 37–38, 46, 77, 89, 153
Teaching, as a profession, 52, 58, 61. See also teachers; training of teachers
Teaching and Learning English as Foreign Language, 139
Teaching ESL Writing, 7
TESOL Quarterly, 6, 8, 88
Test of English as a Foreign Language. See TOEFL
textbooks, 7–8, 50, 51, 71, 89, 92, 163, 166
  and being "textbook-bound," 70, 75, 164–165
  effect of new research on, 99–100
  ineffectiveness in writing instruction, 11, 17, 56, 74, 128, 133
  "Michigan materials," 139–140
  types of, 42, 113–114, 143
thesis statements, 7, 28, 42, 51
Thornton, Liz, 39–40

timed writing, 43, 119
TOEFL, 58
topic selection, 71, 74
topic sentences, 7, 51, 58
total physical response (TPR), 144–145
TPR. See total physical response
training of teachers, 17, 18, 34, 38, 46, 50, 117, 134, 141–142, 164, 166, 169
transitions in writing, 7, 39–40, 98, 100
Truscott, J., 13
tutoring, 77, 168

Understanding ESL Writers, 7–8
Uptaught, 53
Ur, Penny, 17–18

Vocabulary in Context, 139
voice, attention to, in teaching writing, 31, 120n
  student, 113, 114
Vygotsky, Lev, 155

WAC. See writing across the curriculum
writing across disciplines. See writing across the curriculum
writing across the curriculum (WAC), 56, 57, 58, 98, 101, 105, 117
Writing as a Thinking Process, 139
Writing Scientific English, 143–144
writing workshops, 43, 54

Zamel, Vivian, 5, 88, 114, 115, 153